Angels Around Us

What the Bible Really Says

DOUGLAS CONNELLY

CARMEL • NEW YORK 10512

This Guideposts edition is published by special arrangement with InterVarsity Press.

Cover illustration: Roberta Polfus
Designed by José R. Fonfrias
Printed in the United States of America

Library of Congress Cataloging-in-Publication Data
Connelly, Douglas, 1949–
Angels around us: what the Bible really says/Douglas Connelly.
p.   cm.
Includes bibliographical references.
ISBN 0-8308-1695-X
1. Angels—Biblical teaching.   I. Title.
BT966.2.C58   1994
235′.3—dc20 94-3574
CIP

To Paul and Mary Connelly
my parents
and true servants of Christ

Contents

Contents

~ *Acknowledgments* ~

MANY PEOPLE HAVE ENCOURAGED ME in the process of writing this book, but a few (dozen) stand out.

First, the congregation I am privileged to pastor has been extremely supportive. Almost every week someone asks me about "the book." Tom Skaff and Steve Aikman have been my conscience and have kept me accountable. They are true friends.

My editor at InterVarsity Press, Cindy Bunch-Hotaling, has believed in me and in this book from the beginning.

I am most thankful, however, for my little fan club at home—Kim, Kevin, Kyle and my wife, Karen—who have never lost hope in their dad and husband.

My parents, Paul and Mary Connelly, who have modeled Christ before me for over four decades, also deserve great thanks. Their true impact will only be revealed when they stand before Christ and receive abundant rewards from his hands.

Throughout the vast reaches
of God's universe, in a realm unseen
through telescopes or microscopes,
fantastic, powerful beings dwell.

They move at the speed of light
carrying out the commands of their
master. They inhabit the highest heaven,
the atmosphere of earth and the pit
of hell. They are involved in international
political affairs and in the smallest
concerns of children.

These beings are called *angels*.

All the Angels of God

THE EXISTENCE OF ANGELS

NGELS ARE A HOT COMMODITY THESE DAYS. You can find popular books on angels in most local bookstores. In nearly every major city you can take a seminar from people who promise to "put you in touch with your angel." On the national level, *Time, Newsweek* and *USA Today* have devoted front-page cover stories to this current and rising interest.

Unfortunately, most Christians spend very little time thinking about angels. We may acknowledge their existence, but we are usually unaware of their power or their presence in our lives.

Our perception of angels comes primarily from greeting cards and movies. When we think of angels we envision the chubby, naked cherubs who appear each year at Valentine's Day. We recall movies that portray angels as comical characters, like Clarence, the angel in *It's a Wonderful Life*, who tries to get his wings by doing a good deed.

If we happen to think of the biblical angels, it is usually at holidays. We hang the gloria angel above the stable on our nativity set. We sing about angels at Christmas. We read about angels at Easter. But when we are sitting at our desk or working at the store or cleaning house, angels are the farthest thing from our minds.

Yet the Bible offers a surprising amount of information about angels. When I first decided to study them, I carved out three weeks in my calendar for a series of sermons. As I began to study what the Bible had to say, I came to realize the large part angels play in God's program. Eventually the series expanded to a ten-week study, and we had only begun to explore the subject. Even then, the congregation responded with enthusiasm, asking for more.

Seeking a Reliable Source

While the Bible speaks extensively about angels, other sources also claim to provide information about them. In any bookstore's religion or New Age section you will find dozens of books about angels. Some of these books have had a wide and receptive audience.

Most popularly written books contain beautifully drawn figures of angels interspersed with stories of men and women who have encountered angels. These accounts are almost always heartwarming and emotion-laden. I picked up a new angel book this week that begins with three riveting stories—an angel guides a seven-year-old girl through an out-of-body experience, unseen hands pull an electrician from a killer power line, and a hospital patient learns a new lifesaving breathing technique from an angel/nurse.

Many authors tell how to contact your personal angel. Sometimes they give you a series of techniques to follow to get in touch with "the angel within you."

What these New Age angel guides fail to acknowledge is that angels fall into two categories. Good and pure angels do exist, but so do fallen, corrupt angels, who seek to deceive people. Few of the books I have read refer to biblical truth; none point the reader to the salvation and deliverance that comes from Christ alone. Instead these spirit guides counsel you to look into yourself for power (a standard mark of New Age philosophy), or they urge you to link up with a spirit being ("your personal angel").

Any contact with spirits or angels, however, that is not guided by the Holy Spirit and the Word of God is an open door to demonic influence and control. Satan himself can appear to be a sophisticated "angel of light" if it means misleading someone. New Age books on angels are dangerous and unreliable guides.

The writings of other religions claim to give us insight into the angelic realm too. The Apocrypha and later Jewish writings like the Talmud and the Targums provide abundant references to specific angels and angelic involvement in our world. The Qur'an and the theologians of Islam have constructed an elaborate hierarchy of angels. Virtually every religion acknowledges the existence and influence of angels.

But if we cannot trust the writings of other religious groups to tell us the truth about Jesus Christ and his redemptive power, how can we trust what they say about angels? Their speculations may be interesting, but we have no assurance that what we read is the truth.

The only fully reliable source of information about the nature and ministry of angels is the itinerrant Scripture contained in the Bible. The Lord Jesus Christ, whom we as Christians acknowledge as Lord and God, put his stamp of approval on the Old Testament Scriptures he had received and on the New Testament writings his own apostles would produce under the direction of the Holy Spirit (Matthew 5:17-18; John 15:26; 16:13-14). No other body of literature has that mark of authenticity and authority.

Our study in this book will be confined to the Scriptures. The Bible tells us the truth, and we can rely completely on what it declares. Sometimes the Scriptures are silent on questions we would like to have answered. Sometimes only hints or clues are given, and we have to try to piece the clues together. Whatever we conclude, however, about angels—or about any other subject in the realm of God's kingdom—must be based on the Bible's clear declaration. To rely on any other source for information is to stand on shaky ground.

The Biblical Evidence

God has revealed an incredible amount of information about these beings we call angels. Obviously he wants us to know their role in his plan and be aware of their activity in our lives.

Just over half of the biblical books (34 out of 66) refer to angels. Clearly the writers of these books believe that these beings truly exist. Half of the thirty-four books are found in the Old Testament and half in the New Testament. This is no minor doctrine confined to a small corner of the Bible.

The word *angel* appears more than 250 times in the Bible. Our English word comes directly from the New Testament Greek word *angelos*. The corresponding word in the Hebrew Old Testament is *mal'ak*. Both mean "messenger." Occasionally the words are used of a human messenger (1 Samuel 6:21; Luke 7:24; James 2:25), but most often they refer to a heavenly being.

The writers of Scripture use several other terms as well, each highlighting an aspect of the nature or work of angels. God's angels are called his "army" or "host" (Psalm 103:20-21; 148:2; 89:6-8; 1 Samuel 17:45). They are also called "the chariots of God" (Psalm 68:17) because of their swift power and disciplined organization. Daniel describes angels as "watchers" who act as God's agents in the affairs of human government (Daniel 4:13, 17, 23).

The phrase "sons of God" occurs several times in the Old Testament as a general term for all the angels, good and evil (Job 1:6, 2:1; Genesis 6:2). God's angels are called "holy ones" (Psalm 89:7; Daniel 8:13; Zechariah 14:5) and "sons of the mighty" (Psalm 89:6 NASB). At times they even appear bodily as "men" (Genesis 18:2; Acts 1:10).

Final confirmation of the angels' existence comes from the Lord Jesus. During Jesus' earthly life, angels ministered to him in many ways and on several occasions. He repeatedly taught that they would be involved in the climax of human history. When Jesus spoke of the events of the "end of the age," he even claimed personal authority over a group of angels: "The Son of Man will send out *his angels*, and they will weed out of his kingdom everything that causes sin and all who do evil" (Matthew 13:36-41, italics mine).

The witness of the Bible is that angels really do exist. So if you think they belong in the same category as sea monsters, trolls and vampires, think again. Angels are real beings who have a deep interest and involvement in your life.

CHAPTER TWO

Test the Spirits

EVALUATING ANGEL ENCOUNTERS

CHRISTIANS ARE INTERESTED IN THE STORIES of people who have encountered angels. These experiences, in fact, become another source of information. Teaching about angels in seminars or meetings, I have often had someone challenge biblical teaching by saying, "But I had a friend who actually saw an angel, and she told me..."

How can we evaluate individual experiences like these?

In this book I have used a number of personal accounts of encounters with angels, and I've included these to illustrate what the Scriptures teach. As I researched the topic, I read dozens of such reports. I have asked missionaries about experiences on the mission field. Friends have told me stories. People I have never met have called or written to me with angel accounts. Some I have included; many I have not.

In evaluating each account, I have used a simple set of criteria. The primary question I asked is, Does this experience mesh with what the Bible teaches about the nature and ministry of angels?

Some angel stories I rejected because they came from non-Christian sources. Muhammad, for example, claimed to receive the Qur'an directly from the angel Gabriel. Joseph Smith, founder and prophet of the Mormon religion, said that he was led to the golden plates containing the Book of Mormon by the angel Moroni.

I discounted several accounts from Christians because I could not harmonize the experience and the declarations or implications of Scripture. For example, a friend of mine claims that an angel protected him during a series of robberies in his neighborhood. For two nights in a row when my friend came home from work, a dog he had never seen was waiting by his house. Out of kindness, he let the dog in to spend the night. Late the second night, the dog was aroused and began barking. The next day the man learned that several houses around him had been burglarized, but his house had been skipped. He never saw the dog again and is convinced the dog was an angel.

While I believe that God's providential care brought the dog to my friend's home, I have difficulty agreeing that this was an encounter with an angel for one reason: in the biblical record angels never appear to human beings as animals.

On the other hand, some stories about angels correlate well with Scripture. A number of years ago my mother visited a Christian friend of hers who was hospitalized in the intensive care unit. Her friend had been in a serious car accident and was not expected to live. When my mother came into the room one evening, her friend said, "Mary, I'm going to be okay. An angel has been sitting at the foot of my bed all day." I believe this was a valid encounter with an angel for several reasons. First, the angel appeared as a personal being, just as angels consistently appear to humans in the Bible. Second, the encounter was totally unexpected; no psychological or emotional manipulation was involved. The third mark of validity is that the experience harmonizes beautifully with what we read in Scripture about the protective care that angels exercise over believers in Jesus Christ.

God's Providence and Angelic Intervention

Another factor that helps us evaluate personal experiences is an understanding of God's providence. Most Christians would agree that God is actively exercising his care over us as his children. We are God's personal concern. Occasionally God intervenes directly in a believer's life. There is no explanation for what happens except that God did it. Those direct interventions of God are called miracles.

Carol Sintay, a member of our congregation for several years, was diagnosed with a large tumor on her ovary. Her doctors were certain that it was cancerous and that it had grown to include her colon and perhaps other internal organs. Even though Carol was in the middle of a semester in a master's degree program, three surgeons concurred that tne tumor must be removed immediately.

Concerned for Carol, the elders of our church anointed her and prayed for God's healing. When the surgeons opened her body a few days later, they found nothing abnormal. One surgeon, who had seen the tumor on an ultrasound projection *and* on an x-ray, was frantic in his search for it. The other surgeon later asked Carol, "Why didn't you tell us that you had been anointed? We would have rerun the tests." That was a miracle, a divine intervention that cannot be explained in any other way.

God certainly can, and at times does, intervene miraculously in our lives. Most of the time, however, we experience God's care through secondary, indirect means. That indirect care is God's providence.

Farmers understand God's providential care very well. No farmer, at least no successful farmer, lies in bed all morning praying that God will miraculously fill the barns with grain and hay. Instead the farmer works hard to cultivate the ground and to plant the seed. Then he entrusts his work to God's faithful care. The sun and the rains cause the seed to grow and produce a harvest. When the farmer's crops are in, he thanks God for the abundance, but he realizes that God provided the harvest through indirect means.

My son Kevin and I were returning home last summer from a baseball game when a torrential rainstorm broke over us. It was dark, and I could barely see the road ahead. I instantly asked God to help me get home safely. Within seconds I came up behind a semi with a brightly lit array of taillights. We followed the truck's beacon for fifty miles, right to our exit off the expressway. That truck was positioned precisely by the Lord to lead us home, another example of God's providential care.

In contrast, encounters with angels are the *direct* intervention of God through his agents into human affairs. They provide protection, comfort or direction that can't be explained except by a supernatural source.

Struggling with the Issues

Occasionally an angel story seems to fit all the biblical criteria except for one aspect. In some stories the angels say something, usually in an incidental way, that raises questions about their truthfulness.

One striking example involves Robin Naylor, a young woman who in October 1991 gave birth to a baby with a serious chromosomal defect. The baby was sent immediately to another hospital for treatment. When Robin's husband went home to get some much-needed sleep, Robin was left alone in the hospital room to try to sort out her feelings and her future. She felt desolate, as if she were the only person who had ever faced such a trauma.

The next morning a nurse came into Robin's room. She was cheerful and efficient. She introduced herself as Jan and asked Robin if she was going to find it difficult to go home without her baby. Robin responded by sharing some of her struggles. Jan then told Robin that she, too, had had a child with a similar defect and that Robin could feel free to talk to her anytime. As Robin watched Jan, she realized that Jan was leading a normal life even though she had this tragedy in her past. Robin drew strength from the encounter and went home that day encouraged.

When the baby was transferred back to the same hospital, Robin kept watching for Jan so she could tell her how much her words had helped. After several visits to the hospital, Robin asked at the nurses' station when Jan worked. The nurses on duty responded by saying that no one named Jan worked on that floor. Robin even described what the nurse looked like, but no one they knew matched the description.

Several months later, Robin asked to see the hospital records from the days she was in the hospital. On the day of her encounter with Jan an entry on her chart was marked with the initials "J.S." even though no one named Jan was listed on the nurses' roster.

Robin believes that Jan may have been an angel sent to bring encouragement to her at that desperate point in her life. I certainly agree that Jan functioned as a messenger of God's mercy and grace, a frequent ministry of the angels. What raises a flag in my mind, however, is Jan's statement that she had had a baby with a similar genetic problem. From all that we can learn from the Scriptures, angels do not reproduce. How, then, if Jan *was* a ministering angel, could she claim to have had a baby? Was Jan's statement a lie?

I think there is a solution, although it doesn't remove all the questions. Later in this book we will see that angels exercise a special protective ministry over children. It's possible (and this is just my speculation) that Jan had been assigned to care for a child with a problem like Robin's baby's. This caring angel had entered deeply into the experience of loving and nurturing such a child through his or her short life. Perhaps Jan had participated at such a level in the emotion of that experience that she really did understand what Robin was going through that day in the hospital.

As we hear or read personal accounts of encounters with angels, sometimes we may have to suspend judgment on certain aspects of the story. Our responsibility, however, is to *test* the spirits, not *trust* the spirits. God's Word provides the standard against which we are to measure our personal experiences.

Emotion and Culture

We must consider two other key factors when we evaluate experiences with angels: the emotional impact and the cultural background.

First, an encounter with an angel always seems to produce a powerful emotional response. Sometimes the person confronted by an angel feels afraid. At other times a sense of comfort or calm sweeps over them. Almost always those involved in an angelic encounter are left feeling awed. These feelings do not validate the experience, but we should question any encounter in which no emotional response is produced. Angels are magnificent beings, and they never touch our lives without leaving powerful emotional imprints behind.

Second, we have to consider the cultural setting in which the encounter takes place. We often hear about vivid displays of angelic *and* demonic presence in more primitive cultures. When the power of the gospel confronts deeply rooted satanic strongholds in tribal areas, missionaries sometimes must battle spiritual forces openly. In the sophisticated cultures of industrialized nations demons and angels are no less active. They just operate more subtly. A deceiving spirit may come to us in a business suit with a reasonable and even religious argument, but his goal will be the same as the spirit that possesses a tribal shaman—to lead us away from the truth that is in Christ Jesus.

If you feel awkward evaluating the spiritual experiences and claims of other people, listen to the warning of the apostle John:

Dear friends, do not believe every spirit, but test the spirits to see whether they are from God, because many false prophets have gone out into the world. This is how you can recognize the Spirit of God: Every spirit that acknowledges that Jesus Christ has come in the flesh is from God, but every spirit that does not acknowledge Jesus is not from God... We are from God, and whoever knows God listens to us; but whoever is not from God does not listen to us. This is how we recognize the Spirit of truth and the spirit of falsehood. (1 John 4:1-3, 6)

As I have tried to think deeply about the encounters with angels recorded in the Bible and shared from the experiences of other Christians, I have concluded that the appearance of an angel of God to a human being always results in praise and glory to God. A genuine encounter with a genuine angel of God will always move us closer to the Lord and to his truth. If an experience with an angel moves a person away from the truth of God, that experience becomes suspect.

We must evaluate experiences with angels in the light of the clear teaching of God's Word. What we believe has to rest on the "more sure word of prophecy" (2 Peter 1:19 KJV), not primarily on personal experience, because our experiences fade over time. Some people I talk to say, "It was so long ago. It's hard for me to remember exactly what happened." That is not the case with God's truth. The universe may crumble, but the Word of God will never fail.

CHAPTER THREE

Are They Not All Ministering Spirits?

THE NATURE OF ANGELS

STHER MAAS, OR AUNT ET as she is known to dozens of missionary kids around the world, was on her way to church on April 13, 1988. A short distance from home she was involved in a car accident. Her head was cut, and she was bleeding profusely into her eyes. Almost immediately a man came to her and held her arm. At his touch a comforting peace spread over her. The man began shouting orders to people gathering at the scene. His first request was for a box of tissues, with which he dabbed the blood from Esther's eyes. She saw then that he was in his thirties, he wore tan work clothes, and he needed a shave. His next command was for someone to go to a nearby store and call 911. When Esther asked his name, he said he couldn't tell her his name but that she would be fine. The man stayed until the emergency crew arrived and then was gone. No one got his name, and except for this saint of God who needed comfort and care, no one remembered much about him.

When Esther related the story to Christian friends, some of them immediately concluded that an angel had helped her. The man may not have been an angel, of course, but his ministry certainly falls in line with what we know from Scripture as angelic care.

Beyond the fact that they provide help and protection for God's people, what do we know about angels? A veil of mystery surrounds them even after we exhaust all the Bible says regarding them. God gives us some fascinating clues, and we *can* say many things about angels with certainty. But just as much remains hidden.

One fact we can discover is that angels are spirit beings. The writer of the letter to the Hebrews, discussing at length the superiority of Jesus over the angels of God, states, "Are not all angels ministering *spirits* sent to serve those who will inherit salvation?" (Hebrews 1:14, italics mine). So given that angels are spirits, as this author says, we can draw several conclusions about them.

The Question of a Body

Because angels are spirit beings, they do not have physical bodies as we do. The apostle Paul confirms that fact in Ephesians 6:12 when he says that the Christian's spiritual warfare is "not against flesh and blood" but against "the spiritual forces of evil." The real enemies of our souls do not have bodies of flesh and blood. The beings that press the attack against us day after day are spiritual beings.

But the Bible also records several instances in which angels appear in human form, so apparently they can take on physical flesh temporarily. Sometimes angels look so human that they are taken for men. At other times they are clearly angels but have visible, tangible form. In biblical appearances angels always manifest themselves as males, never as women[1] or children. (Biblical cherubs bear no resemblance to chubby, arrow-shooting babies.) Despite their great age, they appear youthful, like the angel at Christ's tomb (Mark 16:5). They also are always clothed, sometimes in brilliant garments (Matthew 28:3; Luke 24:4), sometimes in ordinary clothes (Genesis 19:1, 5).

Angels never take the form of objects, animals or birds, though in Scripture they are sometimes pictured with wings. The prophet Isaiah had a vision of the Lord seated on his throne. Above him were angelic beings called seraphs, who had six wings, two of which were for flight (Isaiah 6:2). Ezekiel describes a vision of four angels called cherubim (the Hebrew plural of cherub) surrounding the chariot-throne of God: "In appearance their form was that of a man, but each of them had four faces and four wings" (Ezekiel 1:5-6; 10:21).

Moses and the craftsmen of Israel obviously knew what winged angels looked like. At God's command they made two cherubim from hammered gold for the cover over the ark of the covenant. One was on each end, and "their wings spread upward, overshadowing the cover" (Exodus 37:6-9). Solomon later had two huge, winged cherubim constructed for the temple and had cherubim carved into the wall panels and doors (1 Kings 6:23-32).

Biblical history may explain in part the almost universal practice of picturing angels as winged creatures. When God drove Adam and Eve from the Garden of Eden, he stationed cherubim at its entrance to keep them away from the tree of life (Genesis 3:24). These angels were visible to anyone who wanted to come to that place. The Garden was destroyed, of course, in the flood, but the description of the winged cherubim would have been passed on into the cultures that developed after the flood. The winged, human-faced bulls of Assyria and the winged sphinxes of Greece may be distant echoes of the cherubim that guarded Eden.

It certainly is possible that *all* angels have wings, but in Scripture, writers usually speak of angels without mentioning them. This may be because we simply are to assume the presence of wings. Or the wings may merely be symbolic of the angels' swiftness. Another possible explanation may be that only particular kinds of angels have wings.

If all angels *do* have wings, however, they may be able to change their appearance to look fully like human beings when God's purposes demand it. When they appear to humans in visible, physical form, they look like men. No wings are folded under their robes.

Appearance in Human Form

Genesis 18 describes one intriguing appearance of angels as men. While camping on the plain of Mamre, Abraham and Sarah were visited by three men. Seeing them, Abraham rushed to greet them and invited them to share his meal. At first Abraham sensed nothing unusual about these men in appearance or behavior. He was simply extending his good will as custom dictated. The three washed their feet with water. They sat down near Abraham's tent and ate curds and milk with some beef that Sarah prepared for them. They looked and acted like ordinary Middle Eastern travelers.

Yet it becomes clear that one of these "men" was the Lord God. The narrator specifically calls him "the LORD" several times (vv. 10, 13, 17). This particular "man" even ordered the other two to rescue Abraham's nephew, Lot, from the city of Sodom before it was destroyed.

As Genesis 19 finally relates, these two were not men either: "The two *angels* arrived at Sodom in the evening, and Lot was sitting in the gateway" (v. 1). Lot took them for travelers. He offered to wash their feet and invited them to his home.

These angels even appeared so much like human males that the men of Sodom desired homosexual relations with them. They demanded that Lot bring the two out of his house (Genesis 19:4-5). Only when Lot protested and the townsmen grew aggressive did the angels reveal their supernatural nature by blinding the men of Sodom. They then took Lot, his wife and their two daughters by the hand and led them safely outside the gates.

All of these acts—eating, washing, walking, holding hands—prove that angels can take a physical human form. This happens many times in the biblical narrative, but it is always a temporary change. Angels, who are spirit beings by nature, do not have physical bodies as we do.

This does not mean, however, that angels are spirit beings in the same sense that God is a spirit being. God the Father is spirit. He has no body. The Bible speaks of God's eyes or God's arm, but in reality God has no physical parts. He is a being unlike any other. He fills the universe with his presence. Angels in contrast are localized. Angels can be present only at one place at one time. Even though they are spirits, angels must move from one place to another. God does not need to move. Everything and everyone is in God's presence.

Invisible Beings

Another conclusion we can draw from the fact that angels are spirit beings is that they are normally invisible to humans. But even though unseen, angels inhabit our world and touch our lives. We will see, for example, that angels observe our worship in the local church. We can't see or hear or sense them directly, but they are present with us nonetheless.

Of course, in two exceptions, angels *can* be seen. First, as concluded above, they can appear in bodily form as men for a time, and then they are visible to anyone near them. Lot saw them, and so did the corrupt men of Sodom. You and I would have seen them if we had been there.

The second exception is that on occasion God allows people to see angels in visions. In visions angels don't assume human form. Instead God allows people to see into the spiritual realm, which normally is invisible to humans.

Balaam the prophet had such a vision (Numbers 22—24). Dreading that the Israelites would conquer his people, as they were doing to many other peoples, Balak, king of Moab, hired Balaam to curse them. While Balaam was on his way to Moab with Balak's men, Balaam's donkey suddenly saw the angel of the Lord standing in the way. The donkey saw the angel; Balaam did not. Finally "the

LORD opened Balaam's eyes, and he saw the angel of the LORD standing in the road with his sword drawn" (Numbers 22:31). God gave Balaam, and no one else except the donkey, the ability to see the angel.

The apostle John's visions recorded in the book of Revelation often included angels. He saw myriads of angels around the throne of God (Revelation 5:11). He also saw seven angels with seven trumpets, and on another occasion a "mighty angel" who was "robed in a cloud, with a rainbow above his head" (Revelation 8:2, 10:1). But, as John says several times, he "saw" these angels while he was "in the Spirit." That is, he saw them in a spiritual vision given to him by God. Had we been with John on the island of Patmos, where he saw these things, we would have seen nothing unusual.

The most dramatic biblical example of this special vision of angels took place when the nations of Israel and Syria (Aram) were at war. The king of Syria decided to capture Elisha, the prophet of the Lord, and he sent his armies to Dothan, Elisha's hometown. Elisha's servant saw the Syrian armies surrounding the city, preparing to attack, and he ran to Elisha in terror. Elisha calmly responded, "Don't be afraid. Those who are with us are more than those who are with them." Then he prayed that God would open his servant's eyes, and when the servant looked, he saw "the hills full of horses and chariots of fire all around Elisha" (2 Kings 6:16-17).

In this situation the angels did not suddenly become human. Instead the servants eyes were opened to see what Elisha had seen and what had been present all along—holy angels of God sent to protect them.

Seeing Angels Today

Among Christians who have had personal encounters with angels, most have found themselves in situations like Lot. They were helped or comforted by someone who appeared to be human but who later could not be found. But occasionally God gives people the kind of insight that Elisha's servant had. In a series of messages about angels, Renald Showers, who is on the staff of the Friends of Israel Gospel Ministry, related this incredible story of angelic protection.

In the early 1950s Mau Mau uprisings spread throughout the African nation of Kenya. The movement protested the colonial domination of the British, but American missionaries were often the targets of brutal attacks too. A group of missionaries with Africa Inland Mission in Kijabe, Kenya, learned of an imminent attack on their mission. Mau Mau warriors moving through the area planned to kill them and any Africans who had believed the Christian message. Thus warned, the missionaries and the African Christians gathered their families onto the mission base. The men decided that they would defend their families as well as they could. They used a few rolls of barbed wire to make a barricade and turned on a few floodlights to illuminate the perimeter of the base. And they waited.

On the night of the expected attack the men put their wives and children in the centermost building and told them to pray. The men stood guard with the few weapons at their disposal. They waited all night, but no attack came. They rejoiced in God's protection, but the full story remained unknown to them.

Several months later one of the missionaries led a captured Mau Mau warrior to faith in Christ. After his conversion the man told the missionary his story. On the night the attack was to be executed, he was among a large contingent of warriors that had surrounded the mission. Just as they were about to attack from all sides, large fiery creatures appeared from out of the night. The creatures stood between the Mau Mau and the missionaries and raced in a circle around the barricade. Frightened by the sight, the warriors fled from the area and refused to return.

The missionaries may not have seen them, but God opened the warriors' eyes to what normally would have been invisible—his band of holy angels. Angels are spirit beings, but occasionally God allows these mighty creatures to step into our realm to render service to those who will inherit salvation.

CHAPTER FOUR

All the Sons of God Shouted for Joy

THE ORIGIN OF ANGELS

UR SON KYLE doesn't let his three-year-old motor idle very long. So it's a treat when at the end of the day he lets one of us rock him for a few quiet minutes. One night I was telling him what a special gift he was and how happy we were that God had given him to us. He was thoughtful for a moment and then asked those questions parents cringe to hear: "Where was I before I was your baby?" and "How did God send me to you?"

The question of origins raises some difficult issues. The Christian community has not come to full consensus on how God created our universe. While we all agree that God was the Creator, his method and timing are still debated.

Similar problems and controversies arise when we talk about the creation of angelic beings. That they were created is accepted as fact. But the method and time of their creation, which the Bible does not precisely define, is still open to debate.

Created Beings

In Psalm 148 the psalmist is calling all of God's universe to praise the Lord.

Praise the LORD from the heavens,
   praise him in the heights above.

Praise him, all his angels,
    praise him, all his heavenly hosts.
Praise him, sun and moon,
    praise him, all you shining stars.
Praise him, you highest heavens
    and you waters above the skies. (vv. 1-4)
Then the psalmist adds:
    Let them praise the name of the LORD,
        for he commanded and they were created. (v. 5)

God spoke, and at his command the angels came into being. The New Testament parallel is Colossians 1:15-16, where the apostle Paul is talking about Jesus Christ, God the Son:

He [Christ] is the image of the invisible God, the firstborn over all creation. For by him all things were created: things in heaven and on earth, visible and invisible, whether thrones or powers or rulers or authorities; all things were created by him and for him.

Jesus Christ brought into existence everything in creation—things in heaven (the realm of angels) and things on earth, the visible things we can see in our realm and the invisible things in the heavenly realm. Angels of every rank were created *by* the Lord Jesus and *for* the Lord Jesus. One command brought millions of angels into being.

Created How?

As we study the Scriptures, we come to understand that angels were made in a unique way. Several clear biblical facts point to the conclusion that each was created directly and individually by God.

First, we know that angels do not reproduce. On one occasion Jesus was arguing with some men about the future resurrection. In the course of the discussion Jesus commented that after our resurrection, we will not bear children. Here's how he stated it: "When the dead rise, they will neither marry nor be given in marriage; they will be like the angels in heaven" (Mark 12:25).

Apparently, angels did not come into being like we did. You and I were not directly created by God. God created Adam directly and individually from the elements of the earth. God created Eve directly and individually from Adam's flesh and bone. But all the rest of us came from Adam and Eve through the process of reproduction. No human being (apart from Jesus) has ever come into existence except by that method. Our bodies and our spirits are derived from our parents. They do not come into existence as the direct creative act of God.

In the future, however, after the resurrection, human beings will not reproduce. We will be like the angels who do not have children. The phrase "neither marry nor be given in marriage" refers as well to the sexual union and reproduction that take place within marriage.[1]

Some Christians have concluded from Jesus' remark that angels have no sexuality. I do not agree with that conclusion. We have abundant evidence that they are males, since in biblical accounts they always appear as males. We will see in a later chapter that they may also function sexually as males, but they cannot reproduce after their own kind as human beings can.

If angels do not reproduce, then each was created as Adam was—individually and uniquely. None was ever born. Angels are called "sons of God" several times in the Bible, but never "sons of angels." They don't have families or ancestors. There are no baby angels, nor do angels grow old. They were all created directly, individually and simultaneously by the all-powerful Creator.

This also means that angels are not the departed spirits of people who have died. God does not make Christians who have died into angels. This idea appears to have sprung from a misreading of Mark 12:25. Jesus does not say that when the dead rise they will *be* angels in heaven. He says they will be *like* angels in this one respect.[2] Human beings remain human beings forever. God created angels as a separate, distinct group of beings in his kingdom.

Jesus makes one further comment on the angels. In Luke 20:36, speaking of people who will be resurrected, he says, "They can no longer die; for they are like the angels." Once the angels were created, they were destined to live forever.

Created When?

Of all the issues related to the origin of angels, the most difficult to settle is the time of their creation.

Jewish scholars through the centuries have been fascinated with the relationship between the angels and the biblical account of creation. One legend says that all the angels were created on the second day. The rabbis, apparently, did not want anyone to think that angels had assisted God in any way with the creation of the heavens and the earth. According to another legend, God created angels on the fifth day, when all the other winged creatures came into being. Agreement on the topic was difficult, of course, but at one time the rabbis did conclude three things about them: all angels walk upright, speak only Hebrew and are endowed with great wisdom.

In some Jewish traditions God even asked the angels' opinion on the creation of humankind. Most were not enthusiastic about the idea. The Angel of Peace opposed man's creation because this new being would be quarrelsome. The Angel of Truth gave the plan a "thumbs down" because man would be full of lies. According to the tradition, the angels who opposed God were consumed by fire.[3]

Most Christian scholars believe that angels existed long before the creation of the earth. According to this view, Satan's fall into sin and rebellion against God took place in the far reaches of eternity past. Some Bible teachers even advocate a long gap of time between the first two verses of Genesis 1, during which Satan's rebellion took place.

I believe, however, that the angels, including Satan, were created more recently than that. When examined together, three passages of Scripture indicate quite clearly how recent that creation took place.

The first clue comes from God's speech to Job and his companions. Having heard Job try to justify himself, God finally answers him and incidentally speaks of when he created angels:

> Where were you when I laid the earth's foundation?
>   Tell me, if you understand.
> Who marked off its dimensions? Surely you know!
>   Who stretched a measuring line across it?
> On what were its footings set,
>   or who laid its cornerstone—
> while the morning stars sang together
>   and all the angels [literally, sons of God] shouted for joy?
>
> (Job 38:4-7)

When God brought the earth into existence, he had an audience. Morning stars sang together, and all the sons of God shouted for joy. Who are these morning stars and sons of God?

The phrase "sons of God" is clearly a title for angels, a fact reflected in the New International translation. In Job chapters 1 and 2 we learn that at times God calls together all the "sons of God" to give an account of their activities. Even Satan is among those called to report. So the phrase "sons of God" is a broad one covering all angels, good and evil.

The other phrase, "morning stars," cannot refer to literal stars because the stars and planets were not created until the fourth day of the creation week. "Morning stars" more likely refers to angels, as Isaiah 14:12-15 indicates. While this passage was written about the king of Babylon, many scholars believe it refers to the angel Lucifer, or Satan, who was originally one of God's most exalted angels:⁴ "How you have fallen from heaven, O morning star, son of the dawn!" (Isaiah 14:12).

The obvious reference of both these phrases in Job 38, "morning stars" and "sons of God," is to angelic beings. The angels watched God create the earth, and they marveled at his power. Since they already existed when God made the earth, they must have been created sometime before then. This is the first clue to the origin of angels.

We find the second clue in a highly unlikely place. When Moses gave God's Ten Commandments to the Israelites, he also established a pattern of six days of labor, then one day of rest—the Sabbath. In explaining that God himself had used that rhythm of life when he created the world, Moses says: "For in six days the LORD made the heavens and the earth, the sea, and all that is in them, but he rested on the seventh day" (Exodus 20:11). The word *them* refers back to the heavens, the earth and the sea. All that exists in those three realms was created by God within the first six days. That certainly includes the angels.

So we know two things about when God created the angels. They were created within the confines of the six days of creation week. And angels were created before the earth was created, because when they saw God bring it into being, they shouted for joy.

The third clue about the angels' origin comes from the first verse of the Bible. God created "the heavens" and then "the earth" (Genesis 1:1). If angels saw God create the earth and if they were created within the six days of creation week, then we must conclude that angels were created on the first day when God created "the heavens."

Putting all the biblical clues together, we can conclude that angels were still newly created when God laid the foundation of the earth on the first day. Angels could respond to that event because they were created as mature, intelligent, fully functional beings. They saw God call the earth into existence by the power of his word alone, and they voiced heavenly praise.

What About That *Old* Serpent, Satan?

Some of you still look skeptical. You are saying, "I've believed that angels were around long before the creation of the earth. And what about Satan? Hadn't he rebelled against God before our world was created?" I believe the answer is no. Satan was created on the first day of creation along with all the other angels. He was created holy and pure, and he shouted for joy with the others when God created the earth. In fact, for the entire six days of that first week, Satan was *still* a holy angel because when God looked at all that he had made up to that point, he saw that "it was very good" (Genesis 1:31).

Satan sinned sometime between the end of the sixth day (Genesis 1:31) and his temptation of Eve in the Garden of Eden (Genesis 3:1). Satan was not an ancient being but a novice. He was created with great beauty and power, but he soon grew proud and rebelled (1 Timothy 3:6). Seeking the worship and adoration for himself that belonged only to God, he set off on a path of deceit and destruction.

Created as What?

Angels were created individually and all at once by God, but we should never think of them simply as the Lord's drones. They are not robots who mechanically carry out his work. God created angels as unique personal beings. They have different personalities just as we humans do. Don't confuse the term *person* with the term *human being*. There are personal beings that are not human beings. God the Father, for example, is a person, but he is not human. Angels are personal beings but not human beings.

Several characteristics of angels mark them as uniquely different personal beings. First, angels demonstrate emotions. We saw earlier in Job 38 that the angels were so joyful at seeing God's creation of the earth that they shouted. A heavenly host of angels praised God at the birth of Jesus, and they rejoice each time a lost person turns to him (Luke 2:13-15; 15:10). While angels express joy, they also express anger. Describing his vision of the future, the apostle John notes Satan's fury when he loses the war in heaven, is cast out and confined to the earth (Revelation 12:12).

Angels also possess intelligence. In the Garden of Eden Satan invades the body of a serpent and tries to persuade humankind to join his rebellion. Satan engages Eve in a conversation that causes her to question God's instruction: "Did God really say, 'You must not eat from any tree in the garden'?" (Genesis 3:1). Such conversation requires reasoning. Personal beings like angels communicate; they use language, they reason, they reach conclusions and they act on those conclusions.

Another mark of personality is the presence of a will, a capacity to make choices. When God created angels, he gave them a will, just as humans have. Satan determined to rebel against God: "I will make myself like the Most High" (Isaiah 14:14). When he persuaded other angels to join him in rebellion, some exercised their wills to follow him. Other angels chose to remain faithful to God.

Personal names also mark angels as distinct personal beings. Three angels are specifically named in Scripture—Gabriel, Michael and Lucifer, or Satan. The Apocrypha and later Jewish and Christian speculation produced hundreds of other angelic names, but Scripture only verifies these three.[5]

Angels have been around a long time. They were created with knowledge, but have grown wiser over their eons of existence. Fallen angels have studied human nature and behavior to sharpen their attack on us. Godly angels use the same insight to come to our aid more effectively. From the beginning of human existence the lines have been clearly drawn. Angels either are under the dominance of God's enemy or are ministers of God's care.

And I Saw a Strong Angel

ANGELS AND POWER

A KEY LEADER OF THE PERSECUTED CHURCH was in prison. Undoubtedly the handful of believers closest to him had discussed rescue attempts, but they were foolish even to try. An army of men could not have successfully stormed the prison. Their pastor was locked in an inner cell on death row, chained to two of the best guards the dreaded secret police could produce. Two others guarded the door. But despite his situation and despite the public execution of another pastor just days before, the man under arrest, called Petros by his flock, slept soundly.

In the quiet of the night an angel appeared in the cell. He woke the pastor with a jab and told him to get up. The chains on his wrists fell off. "Get dressed," the angel commanded. Petros pulled on his clothes and stumbled after the angel as the prison doors opened. At the fearsome iron gate of the prison entrance, no one stopped them. The gate opened without a key. About a block away from the prison the pastor looked back, trying to figure out if this was really happening or if he was only dreaming. When he turned back again, the angel was gone.

This miraculous escape did not take place in the old Communist bloc or in North Korea. It didn't even happen in the twentieth century. It occurred when Petros, whom we know as Peter, was imprisoned by King Herod (Acts 12). This thrilling story of his release shows the extraordinary power of angels. As supernatural beings they have far greater power than we human beings have.

Peter himself made that clear, and since he had more than one encounter with an angel, he should know. In 2 Peter he describes some false teachers who despise authority, even the authority of heavenly beings. Here's what Peter says:

> Daring, self-willed, they do not tremble when they revile angelic majesties, whereas angels *who are greater in might and power* do not bring a reviling judgment against them before the Lord. (2:10-11 NASB, italics mine)

Peter has no doubt that angels are mightier than we are. The Scriptures abound with proof that their power extends into every arena. Angels excel, for example, in wisdom. Having existed since creation, they have a vast reserve of knowledge and experience. When the Old Testament historians wanted to describe King David's profound wisdom, they wrote that he was "like an angel of God in discerning good and evil" (2 Samuel 14:17).

Angels also excel in strength. God repeatedly entrusts his "mighty ones" with amazing duties, which they execute swiftly and powerfully. In the days of David, for example, one angel destroyed 70,000 people in Israel in a single day (2 Samuel 24:15-16). Angels can also afflict people with blindness and strike down arrogant rulers with consuming diseases (Genesis 19:11; Acts 12:23). Of course, not all their feats are gruesome; some are just awesome. Angels can direct the forces of nature, throw great boulders into the sea, and shut the mouths of ravenous lions (Revelation 7:1; 16:5; 18:21; Daniel 6:22).

Even sinful angels possess incredible physical strength. Jesus healed a man possessed by several evil spirits. With the demons controlling him, the man had the power to break chains from his hands and iron shackles from his feet (Mark 5:3-4).

Not only are angels more powerful than humans, but some angels are more powerful than other angels. In his little one-chapter book, Jude talks about the same false teachers that Peter mentioned, but he adds:

These dreamers pollute their own bodies, reject authority and slander celestial beings. But even the archangel Michael, when he was disputing with the devil about the body of Moses, did not dare to bring a slanderous accusation against him, but said, "The Lord rebuke you!" Yet these men speak abusively against whatever they do not understand. (Jude 8-10)

Apparently when Michael went to bury Moses' body, Satan claimed the body for himself. The two angels argued. Michael, an archangel of God, dared not pronounce judgment on Satan, who though fallen, was still more powerful than he. Michael respected Satan's power, so he enlisted an even greater power than either himself *or* Satan by saying, "The *Lord* rebuke you!" Unable to stand against that authority, Satan fled and Michael buried Moses (Deuteronomy 34:6).

I need to add a word here about people who flippantly talk about rebuking or binding Satan. Sometimes these well-meaning folks appeal to their own authority to do that. I've heard people say, "I bind you, Satan, from my children." These people seriously underestimate Satan's power. In our own power we can't take on *any* angel, much less Satan. We certainly shouldn't let ourselves be consumed or paralyzed by his power, but we also can't casually dismiss him this way. According to 1 John 4:4, "The one who is in you is greater than the one who is in the world." I believe that! But Satan remains a formidable foe. We must meet him in the Lord's strength and with the Lord's authority.

Limitations of Angelic Power

While we have to recognize that angels possess supernatural power, we also need to understand that they are not all-powerful. They have some definite limitations.

For example, angels are limited in their presence. One angel cannot be present everywhere at the same time. He is limited to one place at one time. When God sent Gabriel to Mary to announce Jesus' miraculous conception

(Luke 1:26), Gabriel moved from heaven to earth—from the presence of God to the presence of Mary. Satan is not omnipresent; he cannot be in more than one place at a time. Therefore he must gather information using his angels. That is not true of God. Everything, including Satan and his demons, is in God's presence. At times God does choose to work through angels, but he is not dependent on them.

Another limitation on angels is their knowledge. On the occasion when Jesus confronted Legion, the many demons possessing a man, they asked him, "Have you come here to torture us before the appointed time?" (Matthew 8:28-29). Though they knew about their eventual punishment "at the appointed time," they did not know Jesus' immediate intentions toward them.

The great power of angels is limited too. As powerful as Satan is, he and his followers have a final end already determined by God. In the visions recorded in the book of Revelation, the apostle John saw the end of Satan's dominion: "The devil...was thrown into the lake of burning sulfur...[He] will be tormented day and night for ever and ever" (20:10). Please don't ever think of Satan as the king of hell. He isn't. Satan hates hell because that will be his final end. God has dominion over every place, even hell.

God is more powerful than any angel. The Christian faith is not dualistic. We do not see a good God on one side fighting an equally strong evil devil on the other side. We are not waiting anxiously to see which side will win this cosmic battle. The victory already belongs to our God. He is more powerful than Satan and his angels combined. God's power is unlimited; an angel's power is limited. Angels are creatures; God is the Creator.

Warfare in Heavenly Places

While God's victory is secure, we have to realize that the war still continues. Satan is defeated, but he hasn't surrendered. God and his holy angels constantly battle their adversaries, Satan and his evil angels. We usually think of spiritual warfare as the attacks aimed at us Christians, but there is also a continual war among the angels.

Probably no one has done more to raise the Christian consciousness of such warfare than Frank Peretti in his novel *This Present Darkness*. But Daniel chapter 10 offers an equally stunning biblical example. Daniel, after praying and fasting for three weeks about the revelation he had received of a future great war, finally saw a vision of an angel. (This may be Gabriel, who visited him on two earlier occasions [Daniel 8:16-17; 9:21].)[1] The "man," clothed in linen and gold, had gleaming skin and flaming eyes. In awe and exhaustion Daniel fell forward with his face to the ground. The angel touched him and spoke.

> He said, "Daniel, you who are highly esteemed, consider carefully the words I am about to speak to you, and stand up, for I have now been sent to you." And when he said this to me, I stood up trembling.
>
> Then he continued, "Do not be afraid, Daniel. Since the first day that you set your mind to gain understanding and to humble yourself before your God, your words were heard, and I have come in response to them. But the prince of the Persian kingdom resisted me twenty-one days. Then Michael, one of the chief princes, came to help me, because I was detained there with the king of Persia." (10:11-13)

God had immediately heard Daniel's prayer for insight into the revelation. He had even dispatched this angel to answer Daniel's prayer, but the angel had been delayed in reaching Daniel for three weeks. A hostile spiritual power was able to intercept and delay an angel of God for twenty-one days!

Several facts about this hostile power become clear as we think about what the angel told Daniel. First, the being called "the prince of the Persian kingdom" could *not* have been human. No human is able to hinder an angel. Second, since the prince of the Persian kingdom functioned in the realm of angels, he must have been an angel himself. Furthermore, since he opposed one of God's angels, "the prince" must have been one of Satan's angels. A fourth conclusion we can draw is that this evil angel had a specific responsibility. His task was to direct the decisions of the human rulers of Persia. This powerful demonic prince brought his evil influence to bear on the political leaders of a mighty empire.

If we expand that truth to our modern world, it means that demons are actively involved in politics today. They must be using any means they can to influence political leaders who are not controlled by the Holy Spirit. Undoubtedly Satan has appointed a "prince of the United States."

Jesus, of course, knew Satan's powerful status. On one occasion Satan took Jesus to a high mountain and showed him the splendor of the world's kingdoms. Satan offered it all freely if Jesus would bow down and worship him. Oddly, Jesus did not dispute Satan's claim to possess the world's kingdoms. Instead he rebuked Satan for his blasphemous suggestion (Matthew 4:8-10). At another time Jesus called him "the prince of this world," and John adds that "the whole world is under the control of the evil one" (John 12:31; 1 John 5:19).

Since Satan is the prince of this world, we shouldn't be surprised to find his underlings called "princes" of individual nations. No wonder Paul exhorted us to pray fervently for "kings and all those in authority" (1 Timothy 2:1-2). Whether they know it or not, our political leaders are the focus of a spiritual battle. As we saw, the prince of Persia did not want Daniel to receive the angel's interpretation of the vision because that would advance God's plan. Only through the intervention of Michael, a chief prince among God's angels, did this demonic prince lose the skirmish. Daniel's prayers, however, also played some part in this cosmic conflict. Perhaps his continued prayer and fasting provided greater motivation and spiritual power to the angels of God.

One more insight on angelic warfare comes from a statement recorded at the end of Daniel 10. The angel tells Daniel that soon he (the angel) will return to fight against the prince of Persia, and "when I go, the prince of Greece will come" (v. 20). Nations rise and fall at the will of the sovereign God, sometimes as the result of angelic warfare in the unseen realm all around us.

Satan's angels are very strong. Some are strong enough to direct rulers and nations. Some are strong enough to resist (temporarily, at least) the angels of God. Warfare in the angelic realm will reach its climax in the future when Satan and his angels are cast out of the heavenly realms to which they now have access and are confined to the earth (Revelation 12:7-12).

The Battle Against Us

Spiritual warfare is also waged against believers in Christ. In Ephesians Paul commanded, "Be strong in the Lord and in his mighty power. Put on the full armor of God so that you can take your stand against the devil's schemes" (6:10-11). The phrase "the devil's schemes" implies a strategy, a plan of attack. Satan and his angels watch us followers of Christ and make a battle plan based on our weaknesses. Then they diligently pursue that plan in an attempt to defeat us spiritually. Demonic forces know they can't take us back from Christ (Romans 8:38; John 10:28-29), but they can render us ineffective.

Satan's angels are powerful foes. God, however, has not left us defenseless. We have at least four resources, outlined in Ephesians 6, for overcoming the enemy's attacks. The first is the armor of God—spiritual equipment developed as we walk in conscious obedience to him. "Therefore," Paul counsels, since we are engaged in an ongoing spiritual struggle, "put on the full armor of God, so that when the day of evil comes, you may be able to stand your ground" (Ephesians 6:13). God offers us his armor, but it does not automatically shield us. Only by obeying the Lord in our daily life can we avail ourselves of its protection. We can't be careless about how we live and expect protection from demonic attack.

Our second resource in the struggle is "the sword of the Spirit, which is the word of God" (Ephesians 6:17). The only offensive weapon in our armory is a sword—God's Word. As we grow in our understanding of his truth, we become better equipped to strike back. When Satan challenged Jesus in the wilderness, Jesus deflected Satan's attacks by quoting specific Scriptures aimed at the heart of each temptation (Matthew 4:1-11; Luke 4:1-13).

An effective strategy I use is writing out Scripture verses on self-stick notes and putting them where I'm often tempted. You might put Psalm 101:3 on your television screen: "I will set before my eyes no vile thing." Or if Satan attacks your sense of God's provision, Philippians 4:19 or Matthew 6:34 tucked into your checkbook will reassure you. I do know that if you do not have a strategy for rebuking Satan, you will fall for his lies every time!

The most neglected resource in spiritual warfare is prayer. Paul sums up his description of the armor that God provides by saying, "Pray in the Spirit on all occasions with all kinds of prayers and requests" (Ephesians 6:18). Our prayers in times of spiritual struggle or oppression may be short or long, silent or vocal, calm petitions or shrieks of pain, but we *must* pray. Fervent prayer will often leave us exhausted, as it did Daniel, but we can rejoice even in the exhaustion, knowing that our prayers in some way lead to Satan's defeat. In many cases prayer may be our only means of resisting evil. Jesus' disciples once found a demon who refused their commands to leave a young boy. Jesus, after sending the evil spirit away, said, "This kind [of demon] can come out only by prayer" (Mark 9:29).

Our fourth supernatural resource is the Holy Spirit. Paul exhorts us to "pray *in the Spirit*," for through him we can learn the "deep things of God" (Ephesians 6:18; 1 Corinthians 2:10). The Spirit of God, who resides in us, is far wiser and greater than all the enemy's hosts arrayed against us.

Note that none of these four resources seems particularly spectacular. Wearing

God's armor, relying on his Word, praying earnestly and resting in the Spirit require spiritual discipline and a quiet resolve to walk in obedience to God. They may not be included in some of the more exciting testimonies of spiritual warfare heard in church or on Christian television. But these are the resources God has promised to bless. On the other hand, as with Peter's jailbreak, wrought by prayer and the aid of an angel, God's resources can prove spectacular as well as incredibly effective.

Living Out the Truth

The most difficult hours on earth for the Lord Jesus were those spent in Gethsemane just before his arrest and crucifixion. He was in agony. The temptation to turn from the will of the Father was incredibly strong, and Jesus struggled in prayer with loud cries and tears (Hebrews 5:7). But when the struggle in his soul had calmed and Jesus had resolutely determined to continue to the cross, an angel appeared and strengthened him for the torturous hours ahead (Luke 22:43).

I am certain that during our times of spiritual struggle, in response to our earnest and childlike cries, God the Holy Spirit comforts and strengthens us. I know this because God has many times comforted me.

During one particularly dark period in my life, as I was reaping the consequences of disobedience to God, I tended to fall asleep almost immediately at night and awake very early in the morning. In those quiet hours, feelings of failure and condemnation and despair closed around me like a thick black cloud. I could feel Satan's condemning breath in my face. Strongly tempted to abandon my family and my responsibilities, I even devised elaborate plans to run away. More than once I considered suicide. In those desperate months I learned the comfort God can provide. Many times it came through the words and love of my faithful wife, who held and sheltered me as the storms broke over my soul.

Sometimes God's comfort came through friends who took the risk of calling or stopping by to hug me and to tell me they loved me. It may be that occasionally God sent an angel from heaven to strengthen me.

Far too often when we find ourselves under fire, we focus on the attack itself and on the strength of the enemy rather than on the resources available to us. Take heart, Christians! In the dark cavern of despair and pain, the Lord is still with us, and the Spirit is anxious to help us.

Angelic Majesties

THE ORGANIZATION OF ANGELS

MY FAVORITE PART OF THE CHRISTMAS STORY is when the brilliant angel of God appears to a group of shepherds watching their flocks near Bethlehem. I've always been impressed that God bypassed the people of power in Rome and Jerusalem and sent his messengers to people humble enough to receive the announcement of the Savior's birth. One angel delivered the message, but before he left "a multitude of the heavenly host" joined him, praising God and shouting, "Glory to God in the highest, and on earth peace, good will toward men" (Luke 2:13-14 KJV).

If you went through the Bible from cover to cover, you would discover that nowhere does it say exactly how many angels exist. But several passages make it clear that the angels are an enormous host. In Revelation 5, for example, John is taken to heaven in a vision, and he records seeing great numbers of angels around God's throne: "Then I looked and heard the voice of many angels, numbering thousands upon thousands, and ten thousand times ten thousand" (Revelation 5:11). Ten thousand times ten thousand is 100 million! John saw that many plus thousands more. Like John, the Old Testament prophet Daniel also saw into heaven, and he used the same language to describe the angelic host: "Thousands upon thousands attended him [the Ancient of Days]; ten thousand times ten thousand stood before him" (Daniel 7:10).

These visions indicate that angels number in the hundreds of millions. Yet in the Bible those who encounter angels normally see just one or two at a time. Only in

rare instances, as with the angelic multitude on the night of Jesus' birth, do people
see many angels. Outside the biblical experiences, a fortunate few may see or hear a
group of them. For example, during the revival in Wales in 1904, some Welsh
Christians reported hearing choirs of angels singing praise to God.

With so great a multitude, some sort of order becomes necessary. Throughout
the Bible God's angels are collectively called "the host of the Lord" or "the
heavenly host." "Host" translates from the Old Testament Hebrew word *tsaba* and
the New Testament Greek word *stratia*. Both mean a well-trained army, one that
is prepared for war (1 Samuel 17:20, 45; Revelation 19:19). So God's angels are
not a mob but a disciplined army with "the Lord of hosts" as their leader.

While Scripture never clearly lays out the precise structure, this army of
angels evidently makes use of ranks and divisions, where some angels and groups
of angels direct others. Early Christian theologians tried to work out a ranking of
the angels. St. Ambrose, St. Jerome, Gregory the Great and John of Damascus
each proposed a scheme. Thomas Aquinas finally settled on a nine-level
hierarchy, listed here in descending order of authority: seraphim, cherubim,
thrones, dominations (or dominions), powers, virtues, principalities, archangels,
angels.[1] The Roman Catholic Church accepted Aquinas's list as dogma. Protestant
theologians, however, have tended to reject it, primarily because there is no
direct scriptural support for it.

We may not know how the ranks of angels relate to each other, but we do
have amazing information about certain categories of angels. If we can appreciate
this elaborate system of authority and order among them, which God has
developed, we will be less likely to treat them casually. For far from being a
superficial afterthought of God, angels are an integral part of his active reign
over creation. They respond as soldiers under a general's command, their loyalty
unquestioned, their obedience instantaneous.

Seraphs

Isaiah the prophet saw a vision of God seated on his throne in the temple (Isaiah 6). Flying above him were astonishing beings called seraphs (the Hebrew plural is *seraphim*, since adding *-im* to a Hebrew word makes it plural). The word literally means "burning ones," for these angels dwell so closely to the presence of God that they burn with his holy brilliance. The seraphs, as Isaiah describes them, have six wings. Two wings cover their faces in reverence; two cover their feet in humility; two propel them back and forth above the Lord. The seraphs also have humanlike features: feet, hands (one angel carried a burning coal from the altar "in his hand" and touched it to Isaiah's lips), and voices that shook the doorposts. They called back and forth, announcing the Lord's holy character, and one pronounced cleansing and forgiveness to Isaiah (v. 7). Seraphs are obviously majestic, pure, powerful beings.

No other angels are called seraphs in Scripture. It is possible, however, that the apostle John saw them in his vision of God's throne recorded in Revelation 4. The beings John saw did not fly above the throne but stood around it. He describes four "living creatures" that were covered with eyes, a symbol of their knowledge and unending vigilance in God's service. These beings each had six wings, and, like the seraphs in Isaiah 6, they constantly declared the purity of God: "Holy, holy, holy is the Lord God Almighty, who was, and is, and is to come" (Revelation 4:8). Even the angels closest to God's glory recognize that he is set apart and infinitely greater than his Creation.

Cherubs

Another rank or level of angels is cherub. The word *cherub* comes from a Hebrew root word that means "to plow" or "to till the ground." This original farming term came to imply diligent service. Like seraphs, cherubs are angels that stand close to God's throne, prepared to do his bidding at a moment's notice.

Ezekiel the prophet gives us the clearest description of a cherub. They don't resemble even vaguely the pudgy, naked Valentine babies we usually think of as cherubs. Instead Ezekiel saw four beings that surrounded and supported God's throne:

I looked, and I saw a windstorm coming out of the north—an immense cloud with flashing lightning and surrounded by brilliant light. The center of the fire looked like glowing metal, and in the fire was what looked like four living creatures. In appearance their form was that of a man, but each of them had four faces and four wings. Their legs were straight; their feet were like those of a calf and gleamed like burnished bronze. Under their wings on their four sides they had the hands of a man. All four of them had faces and wings, and their wings touched one another. Each one went straight ahead; they did not turn as they moved.

Their faces looked like this: Each of the four had the face of a man, and on the right side each had the face of a lion, and on the left the face of an ox; each also had the face of an eagle. Such were their faces. Their wings were spread out upward; each had two wings, one touching the wing of another creature on either side, and two wings covering its body. Each one went straight ahead. Wherever the spirit would go, they would go, without turning as they went. The appearance of the living creatures was like burning coals of fire or like torches. Fire moved back and forth among the creatures; it was bright, and lightning flashed out of it. The creatures sped back and forth like flashes of lightning. . . .

Spread out above the heads of the living creatures was what looked like an expanse, sparkling like ice, and awesome. Under the expanse their wings were stretched out one toward the other, and each had two wings covering its body. When the creatures moved, I heard the sound of their wings, like the roar of rushing waters, like the voice of the Almighty, like the tumult of an army. When they stood still, they lowered their wings.

Then there came a voice from above the expanse over their heads as they stood with lowered wings. Above the expanse over their heads was what looked like a throne of sapphire, and high above on the throne was a figure like that of a man....This was the appearance of the likeness of the glory of the LORD. (Ezekiel 1:4-14, 22-26, 28)

We know that the beings Ezekiel saw were cherubs because in another vision he sees them again and specifically identifies them as cherubs: "These were the living creatures I had seen beneath the God of Israel by the Kebar River, and I realized that they were cherubim" (Ezekiel 10:20).

From Ezekiel's vision we get a fairly detailed description of cherubim. First, their appearance is basically human, but each one has four faces, resembling a man, a lion, an ox and an eagle. They have human hands, but they also have four wings. In the vision two wings cover their bodies in reverence before God. The other two wings are outstretched so that their tips touch the wingtips of angels on each side. When they use these two wings to move or to fly, they create a tumultuous sound.

As the Old Testament records, God chose to use the image of these striking beings in the tabernacle, his designated dwelling place among the people of Israel. At God's instruction two golden cherubs were placed on the mercy seat, the lid of the ark of the covenant (Exodus 25:18-20). The cherubs faced each other from opposite ends of the ark with wings stretched out; "enthroned between the cherubim" was God's visible outshining (Psalm 80:1; 1 Samuel 4:4; 2 Kings 19:15; 1 Chronicles 13:6; Psalm 99:1). Weavers also worked cherubim designs into tapestries for the tabernacle (Exodus 36:8, 35). Later in Solomon's temple, craftspeople carved the designs into walls and doors and constructed huge figures of them (1 Kings 6:23-35). In his vision of the future temple Ezekiel saw similar carvings that covered the walls from top to bottom (Ezekiel 41:17-20).

God may have chosen to decorate his temple with cherub designs because that reflects their actual role of serving in his presence. Unlike other angels, they never convey instructions or messages to human beings; not once are they directly called "angels" or messengers. With the single exception of those who guarded the entrance to the Garden after Adam and Eve left, cherubs are always found in God's immediate presence, protecting his throne and reflecting his glory (Genesis 3:24). God, of course, does not need the protection of his creatures, but the cherubim around God's throne declare his transcendence and unapproachable majesty. The Lord, the psalmist wrote, "mounted the cherubim and flew; he soared on the wings of the wind" (Psalm 18:10).

Probably the most startling fact about cherubim is that God's highest cherub was Satan. We learn this from Ezekiel's poetic curse in Ezekiel 28. In the first part of the chapter the sovereign Lord addresses a message to the proud human "ruler" (Hebrew *nagid*) of the Phoenician city of Tyre, located north of Judah. The curse is clearly directed to a man (v. 9). But in verse 12 God begins to talk to the "king" (Hebrew *melek*) of Tyre, the real ruler, Satan himself.

You were the model of perfection,
    full of wisdom and perfect in beauty.
You were in Eden,
    the garden of God;
every precious stone adorned you....
Your settings and mountings were made of gold;
    on the day you were created they were prepared.
You were anointed as a guardian cherub,
    for so I ordained you.
You were on the holy mount of God;
    you walked among the fiery stones.
You were blameless in your ways
    from the day you were created

till wickedness was found in you.
Through your widespread trade
   you were filled with violence,
   and you sinned.

So I drove you in disgrace from the mount of God,
   and I expelled you, O guardian cherub,
   from among the fiery stores.
Your heart became proud
   on account of your beauty,
and you corrupted your wisdom
   because of your splendor.
So I threw you to the earth;
   I made a spectacle of you before kings.

(vv. 12-17)

Satan was the most beautiful and powerful of all God's angels—the "guardian cherub." Perhaps he held the honorable and holy place closest to God's presence. But because he was the highest "model of perfection," Satan thought he could be like God in nature. He didn't properly recognize his beauty and splendor as gifts from God, so they became sources of pride and instruments of rebellion.

Archangels

A third category of angels appears only twice in the Bible. Archangels are first mentioned in a letter to the Thessalonians, where it states that Jesus will return for his church "with a loud command, with the voice of the archangel, and with the trumpet call of God" (1 Thessalonians 4:16). The second mention is more specific; in Jude 9 the angel Michael is called "*the* archangel."

Michael often acts as the defender of Israel. One angel, speaking to Daniel the prophet, describes Michael as "your prince" and "the great prince who protects your people" (10:21; 12:1). Michael also seems to be the supreme military leader of the angelic army, because it is he and "his angels" who will eventually remove Satan and his angels from heaven (Revelation 12:7-10).

Michael is the only angel referred to in the Bible as an "archangel," and he may be the only one. In Daniel 10:13, however, Michael is said to be *one* of the chief princes." It is possible that other archangels exist but are not named in Scripture. Some Bible scholars believe that "the seven angels who stand before God" (Revelation 8:2) are archangels. This is substantiated by *I Enoch*. Written by a Jewish author about 100 b.c., this long book names seven archangels: Michael, Gabriel, Uriel, Rague, Seraquel, Haniel and Raphael.[2]

In writings outside the Bible, no individual angel has gained the prominence of Michael. He ranks as the greatest of all angels, whether in Christian, Jewish or Islamic literature. The Jews identify Michael as the angel who destroyed the invading army of Sennacherib (2 Kings 19:35). They also believe that Michael was the angel who held back the arm of Abraham as he was about to sacrifice Isaac. In the War Rule, a scroll found among the Dead Sea Scrolls, Michael is the "Prince of Light" who leads the angels of light into battle against Belial and the angels of darkness.[3] In Christian legend Michael was sent to Mary, the mother of Jesus, to announce her approaching death.

In the Western world Gabriel and Michael are the angels most often depicted in religious pictures and icons. Artists usually portray Michael as a winged man with an unsheathed sword—the warrior of God and the slayer of the Dragon. Milton, Dante and Longfellow all included Michael in their writings, and William Butler Yeats in his poem "The Rose of Peace" called him the "leader of God's host."[4]

Gabriel

Besides Michael and Lucifer, the only other angel designated by a personal name in the Bible is Gabriel. His name means "mighty one of God," and Luke calls him "an angel of the Lord" (Luke 1:11). Gabriel describes himself as one who "stand[s] in the presence of God" (Luke 1:19). Gabriel's most common responsibility, as recorded in the Bible, is to bring messages of vital importance to God's servants. Looking like a man, he came "in swift flight" to Daniel to impart insight and understanding (Daniel 8:15; 9:21-22). He was the angel who announced the birth of the Messiah's forerunner to the old priest Zechariah (Luke 1:19). It was also Gabriel who was privileged to tell Mary that she would bear the Son of God (Luke 1:26-38). Whenever Gabriel appears in Scripture, he is the special messenger of God who brings important news about Israel and the Messiah.

As with Michael, Gabriel has found his way into extrabiblical literature. Muhammad claimed that it was Gabriel (Jibril in Arabic) who dictated the Qur'an to him, word by word, chapter by chapter. Some Jewish sources credit Gabriel with the rescue of Shadrach, Meshach and Abednego from the fiery furnace (Daniel 3:25,28). In John Milton's *Paradise Lost*, Gabriel is chief of the angelic guards of Paradise.

Special Groups and Ranks of Angels

Two New Testament passages seem to indicate other ranks of angels. Colossians 1:16 says,

> For by him [Christ] all things were created: things in heaven and on earth, visible and invisible, whether *thrones* or *powers* or *rulers* or *authorities*.

In the invisible realm of angels, just as in the visible realm of humanity, there are levels of authority and rank. The apostle Paul indicates the same truth in Ephesians 6:12, where he writes:

For our struggle is not against flesh and blood, but against the *rulers*, against the *authorities*, against the *powers* of this dark world and against the spiritual forces of evil in the heavenly realm.

All the terms I have emphasized refer to positions of rule and authority. Within both God's kingdom and Satan's dominion, among holy angels and among fallen angels, there are varying levels of authority and power (Ephesians 3:10; Colossians 2:10).

While we have enough evidence to say that there are distinct ranks of angels, not enough biblical information exists to make a complete organizational scheme. Despite sincere efforts by some theologians in the past to define precise ranks, all their conclusions are speculation at best.

In addition to ranks, the Scriptures identify certain groups of angels who have specific functions. John, in the book of Revelation, for example, talks about "four angels standing at the four corners of the earth, holding back the four winds of the earth" (7:1). He also saw "seven angels who stand before God" and sound trumpets (8:2) and seven angels "with the seven last plagues" who came out of the temple (15:1).

John also remarks on individual angels in his Revelation. An angel with a sharp sickle (14:17), an angel "who had charge of the fire" (14:18) and the angel "in charge of the waters" (16:5) play parts in God's final judgment. An unusual angel appears in Revelation 9:11. He is called "the angel of the Abyss," and he rules as king over the demonic forces released from the abyss (9:11). His name is Abaddon in Hebrew and Apollyon in Greek; both words mean "destroyer." This is either Satan or a powerful evil angel under Satan's control. But neither Satan nor any of his angels reign anywhere as king for long. One of God's angels comes "down out of heaven, having the key to the Abyss and holding in his hand a great chain." This angel seizes Satan and binds him for a thousand years (20:1-2).

An Army Around Us

Not only are the angels of God organized as a great army, but they often appear to human beings as mighty warriors of the Lord. They come to our aid as a strong host. I've already related a couple of instances both from the Bible and from modern times in which angels manifested themselves as an army. There is one other account that I've remembered for many years. When I was a teenager, a missionary who visited our church challenged me to read the autobiography of John Paton. The book had been written almost a century before, but the pages gripped my attention and my heart.

In 1858 John Paton and his wife went from Scotland to the New Hebrides, islands in the southern Pacific. At nearly every step of their ministry, demonic forces and the native people under their control tried to silence Paton's proclamation of the gospel. On one occasion a large band of natives surrounded the missionary compound, with the intention of burning it and killing Paton and his wife. The Patons prayed all night. By morning the attackers were mysteriously gone, without having harmed them. The Patons were puzzled, but they praised God for his deliverance.

Over the next months of faithful ministry, the chief of the local tribe became a believer in the Lord Jesus. When John Paton asked what had kept him from attacking, the chief told him that they had seen many men standing around the compound. There were hundreds of them, dressed in brilliant garments with sharp swords in their hands. John Paton realized then that God had sent a contingent of the heavenly army to protect his servants from attack.[5]

The Devil and His Angels

THE CORRUPTION OF ANGELS

N GHOST, A POPULAR ROMANTIC MOVIE made in 1990, a mugger shoots and kills a young man who is out on a date with his girlfriend. The man's body dies, but his spirit lives and remains on earth. He is invisible to human beings but visible to other human spirits also living on earth. He communicates with his girlfriend through a "channel"—a fortuneteller who claims to have contact with the spirit world. Eventually the hero solves the plot behind his own murder, gives his girlfriend one final "kiss" and leaves the earth.

All this makes the movie very romantic, but from a biblical viewpoint these ideas present some serious problems. The screenwriters, however, did get one theological point right—well, almost right. When it came time for the human spirits to depart from the earth, those who were good in character were escorted upward by beings of light. Those humans who had been evil were swarmed upon by dark shadowy figures and dragged down into the cosmic sewers.

Good angels certainly exist—but so do evil angels. Most contemporary books on angels and most New Age angel guides say very little about evil angels. Some instructors and seminar leaders absolutely deny their existence. In my opinion that is one of the great dangers of the modern angel movement. The Bible clearly declares that angels fall into two distinct groups—holy angels of God and evil angels. Satan and the evil angels will transform themselves into what seem to be angels of light if they can use that masquerade to lead undiscerning people away from Christ (2 Corinthians 11:14). Jesus called Satan "a liar and the father of lies" (John 8:44). That's why the apostle John commands us to "test the spirits," not trust the spirits. Those who profess to teach us about the world of angels should be measured by the standard of God's truth.

The questions I want to explore in this chapter are, How did moral evil enter the angelic realm? and, What effect has it had on these marvelous, powerful beings who were designed to serve God?

When God made the angels, he created them all as holy angels. God is not the source of moral evil, so everything that he created was originally "good" in the fullest sense of the word (Genesis 1:31). The angels, however, were untested in their holiness. Their loyalty to God was unchallenged until one powerful angel allowed pride to enter his heart. That angel failed the test of loyalty and rebelled, and in his rebellion he put all the other angels to the test. Would they be loyal to God or would they follow the rebel?

The Day-Star Falls

The original angel to rebel against God was the most powerful and most beautiful of all the angels—the anointed cherub who dwelled above the throne of God. In the Authorized or King James Version of the Bible, the angel's name is translated as Lucifer. The word *lucifer* is Latin for "light-bearer." It found its way into the English Bible by way of the Latin Vulgate. In Hebrew the angel's name was Helel, which means "shining one" or "day-star."

Lucifer, like all the angels, was created during the first day of creation week. He saw God lay the foundations of the earth and rejoiced as God formed the universe. At least through the six days of creation week Lucifer maintained his place of honor and glory. But shortly after the sixth day, that same honor and glory overflowed into pride.

Isaiah the prophet poetically describes Lucifer's change of focus from God to himself.[1] Isaiah begins by taking up a "taunt against the king of Babylon," but as he thinks about the king's condemnation to hell, his mind turns for a few lines to the evil master behind the wicked human king (14:3, 9-11). Isaiah takes up a taunt against Satan himself:

> How you have fallen from heaven,
> O morning star, son of the dawn!
> You have been cast down to the earth,
> you who once laid low the nations!
> You said in your heart,
> "I will ascend to heaven;
> I will raise my throne
> above the stars of God;
> I will sit enthroned on the mount of assembly,
> on the utmost heights of the sacred mountain.
> I will ascend above the tops of the clouds;
> I will make myself like the Most High."
> But you are brought down to the grave,
> to the depths of the pit. (14:12-15)

Lucifer became so proud of his beauty and position that he deceived himself into thinking that he could actually overthrow the sovereign Ruler of the universe. He thought he could replace God or at least rise to a level equal with him. His goal was to be just like God. To accomplish that Lucifer had to either raise himself to God's level or somehow bring God down to his. He has been trying to do both ever since.

That proud moment when Lucifer said in his heart, "I will make myself like the Most High," he fell into moral sin. He stopped being a holy angel, and he became an evil angel. His power was intact. His beauty was intact. He lost his exalted position, of course, but he was determined to make his own way in the universe. He would raise his own throne "above the stars [angels?] of God" (14:13). So Lucifer, "the day-star," became Satan, which means "the enemy, the adversary." His nature was totally corrupted with evil.

One of the toughest philosophical questions surrounding our faith is the problem of evil. If God is good and if God's creation is good, where did evil come from? When Adam and Eve sinned in the Garden of Eden, there was a tempter to lead and deceive them. When we sin, we have three enemies encouraging us: "the world" provides the opportunity for sin, "the devil" plays on our weaknesses, and our own sinful bent, "the flesh," rises up and urges us on.

But Satan had no sinful world to lure him, no tempter to push him and no innate sinful nature to overpower him. Where, then, did moral evil originate? The Bible doesn't explain except to say that, just as sin entered the human race through Adam, sin entered the angelic realm as rebellious pride was born in the will and in the heart of one angel.

Satan's Kingdom

Because God has a kingdom, Satan (if he was going to be like God) needed a kingdom too. In God's kingdom, God ruled over both angelic and human subjects. So Satan set out to fill his kingdom with both angelic and human subjects. Satan, however, had a problem. God had the ability to create personal subjects. Satan, as a creature of God, did not have the ability to create personal subjects. The most Satan could hope for was to persuade or deceive some of God's angels and some of God's humans to join him.[2]

Genesis 3 describes Satan's deception of human beings very clearly. Like the angels, our parents, Adam and Eve, were created in a state of untested holiness. God placed one test in the garden. They were not to eat of the tree of the knowledge of good and evil (Genesis 2:16-17). Yet Satan, disguised as a serpent, persuaded Eve to eat its fruit. Eve offered some to Adam, and he also ate. They failed God's test, and as a result they became sinners. By corrupting human nature at the very beginning, Adam and Eve plunged the human race into sin (Romans 5:12, 17). It is only through Christ's redemptive power that we are made part of God's kingdom (Colossians 1:13).

Satan's deception of other angels is not described in Scripture, but we know that other angels followed him. God apparently allowed Satan to approach and to test the other angels. Many were deceived and followed Satan. We don't know whether all the angels were tested at one time or whether it is possible today for a holy angel to become sinful. I am inclined to believe that angels can still fall. We do know that, by the time Satan is cast out of heaven and confined to the earth in the future, one-third of the angels will have chosen to follow him. In Revelation 12:4 John sees Satan as a great dragon that sweeps "a third of the stars [angels] out of the sky." A number of times we read about Satan and his angels (Matthew 25:41; Revelation 12:7, 9). Satan has a large number of angels under his control, doing his work, according to his will.

Those angels who follow Satan experience a "fall" away from God and into a state of sin just like Satan did. They are confirmed in their sinfulness. In contrast, the angels who pass the test and who maintain their loyalty to God are confirmed in their holiness.

We have in existence, then, two clearly distinct groups of angels. On one side we have the good angels, the holy angels of God. Paul, in 1 Timothy 5:21, calls them God's "elect angels." On the other side we have fallen angels, Satan's angels. They are also called "demons." Some Bible teachers have tried to make a distinction between demons and fallen angels, but I don't think it is possible. Satan is called "the prince of demons" (Matthew 12:24; Luke 11:15). Demons, evil spirits and Satan's angels are all the same beings.

Satan's Angels

Angels operating under Satan's direction are engaged in a number of activities. Their major function certainly is to "demonize" human beings. Toward unbelievers, their activity may range from temptation to sin to oppression.

Demons may actually dwell in some unbelievers and control them. For example, when Jesus came by boat to the country of the Gerasenes, he was confronted by a terrifying man.

When Jesus got out of the boat, a man with an evil spirit came from the tombs to meet him. This man lived in the tombs, and no one could bind him any more, not even with a chain. For he had often been chained hand and foot, but he tore the chains apart and broke the irons on his feet. No one was strong enough to subdue him. Night and day among the tombs and in the hills he would cry out and cut himself with stones.

When he saw Jesus from a distance, he ran and fell on his knees in front of him. He shouted at the top of his voice, "What do you want with me, Jesus, Son of the Most High God? Swear to God that you won't torture me!" For Jesus had said to him, "Come out of this man, you evil spirit!"

Then Jesus asked him, "What is your name?"

"My name is Legion," he replied, "for we are many." And he begged Jesus again and again not to send them out of the area.

A large herd of pigs was feeding on the nearby hillside. The demons begged Jesus, "Send us among the pigs; allow us to go into them." He gave them permission, and the evil spirits came out and went into the pigs. The herd, about two thousand in number, rushed down the steep bank into the lake and were drowned.

Those tending the pigs ran off and reported this in the town and countryside, and the people went out to see what had happened. When they came to Jesus, they saw the man who had been possessed by the legion of demons, sitting there, dressed and in his right mind; and they were afraid. (Mark 5:2-15)

Twice more, as the passage continues, this man is said to be "demon-possessed" (vv. 16, 18). He was controlled not just by one but by many demons. When he spoke, they used the man's vocal chords to speak in audible tones. The man was demonized to the point of complete control.

I will warn you, as I have earlier in this book, that demons are stronger than we are. Only the authority of Jesus Christ can overcome a demon who oppresses someone.[3]

Toward believers, demons function in several ways. First, demons wage war against us. As Paul says, we are in a struggle against spiritual forces of evil (Ephesians 6:12). Second, demons seek to deceive us. Paul warned Timothy that deceiving spirits bring with them things taught by demons (1 Timothy 4:1). As I noted earlier, Satan will disguise himself as an angel of light if that will lead someone astray. Demons also seek to oppress and defeat believers. In 2 Corinthians 2:11 Paul says that we are not to be ignorant of Satan's schemes. Satan and his angels look us over very carefully. They lay cunning plans against each of us, and if we aren't walking in the Spirit, we will fall.

I do not believe it is possible for a Christian to be demon-possessed. We are indwelt by the Holy Spirit, and he will not allow a demon to control us. But to the degree that we open ourselves to it, we as Christians can be demonized and oppressed. When we give Satan a foothold through sin or carelessness, he gains wider and wider access to our lives. The answer to demonic oppression for a Christian is the same as it is for an unbeliever—the power of Christ and the spiritual resources God has given us.

Satan's Realm of Operation

If you've always believed that Satan and his angels have hell as their base of operations, your theology comes more from "The Far Side" cartoons than from the Bible. As strange as it may sound, demons inhabit the heavens. The Bible uses the word *heaven* in three ways. The first heaven is the air, the atmosphere around the earth. Jesus in Matthew 6:26 said, "Look at the birds of the air [literally, of the heaven]." Birds fly in the first heaven. The second heaven is what we call space. Psalm 8:3 says, "When I consider your heavens…the moon and the stars." The third heaven is the place where God dwells. When Stephen, the first Christian martyr, was being stoned, he "looked up to heaven and saw the glory of God, and Jesus standing at the right hand of God" (Acts 7:55). The third heaven is the place where Jesus is, the place where God dwells (see 2 Corinthians 12:2). It is also the habitation of the holy angels. They surround God's throne, waiting to be sent on any mission God desires. They have access to earth, but they dwell in God's presence.

The fallen angels do not dwell in God's heaven. Before his fall Lucifer did live on "the holy mount of God," but he was driven from that exalted place (Ezekiel 28:14-16). Based on the biblical evidence we have, Satan and his angels dwell primarily in the first heaven—in the atmosphere of the earth. Several passages of Scripture lead to that conclusion. First, in Ephesians 2:2, Paul describes Satan as "the ruler of the kingdom of the air." Satan (and, by inference, his demons) operates in the realm of the first heaven. That view is supported by a statement Jesus made to one of the seven churches to which the book of Revelation was addressed. To the church in Pergamum he said, "I know where you live—where Satan has his throne…where Satan lives" (Revelation 2:13). Satan undoubtedly has a place in the earthly realm where he lives even today.

Another key passage is in Job chapter 1. God called all the angels together to give an account before him, and Satan was among them. God addressed him, "Where have you come from?"—implying that Satan came from another place. Satan answered, "From roaming through the earth and going back and forth in it." Satan's dwelling place is the earth and the air or atmosphere around the earth.

I need to add one word of caution. Some Christians have pressed Satan's dominion over the "air" too far. When radio broadcasts and again when television broadcasts began, many Christians said these media were satanic because the signals came through the air. There's no doubt that some radio and television broadcasts are satanic, but it is not because the signals pass through Satan's domain. The problem is in the hearts of those who write and produce the programs.

Besides showing that Satan's domain has changed from the heavens to the earth, this example from Job shows something else: Satan still has access to God's heaven. He can enter God's presence under two circumstances. First, God may require Satan to appear before him as we saw in Job (Job 1:6-7; 2:1-2). Even in his sinful state, Satan is accountable to God!

When I was teaching this truth in a seminar on angels, one woman objected strongly to the idea that Satan could enter God's presence. She based her objection on Habakkuk 1:13—"Your [the Lord's] eyes are too pure to look on evil." How, this woman wondered, could God look on Satan? My response was twofold. First, the verses in Job say that God calls Satan into his presence and that he carries on extended conversations with Satan. Second, since the Bible repeatedly says that God observes evil and evil workers and evil angels, what Habakkuk must have meant is that God cannot look on evil *with approval*. The New American Standard translation brings out exactly that idea: "Thine eyes are too pure to approve evil, And Thou canst not look on wickedness with favor." God certainly sees everything—good and evil—but he cannot look at evil or at an evil being and pronounce it good. God is nauseated by Satan and by Satan's evil (see Psalm 5:4-5).

Satan also has access to God's heaven when he wants to accuse a believer before God. Revelation 12 describes Satan's future confinement to the earth, but we are also told something interesting about his activity in God's heaven:

The great dragon was hurled down—that ancient serpent called the devil, or Satan, who leads the whole world astray. He was hurled to the earth, and his angels with him.

Then I heard a loud voice in heaven say:

"Now have come the salvation and the power and the kingdom of our God,
and the authority of his Christ.
For the accuser of our brothers,
who accuses them before our God day and night,
has been hurled down." (vv. 9-10)

Satan accuses us before God "day and night." That phrase can mean "continually" or it can mean "at any time." I prefer the second meaning. Satan lives on the earth and in the air. He roams about watching for opportunities to deceive and destroy, and he has access to God's presence any time as an accuser of believers.

What a depressing thought! I'm sure Satan is kept pretty busy just raising accusations about me to God! But what a comfort and encouragement it is to know that in God's presence continually and eternally is my High Priest, Jesus Christ (Hebrews 9:12). When Satan brings an accusation, we have an advocate, a defense lawyer, who pleads our case before the Father and who intercedes for us on the basis of his death as our substitute (1 John 2:1-2; Hebrews 10:10, 12, 14). Since God has declared himself to be for us, who can stand against us? Who can bring any charge against God's elect? We are more than conquerors through him who loved us (Romans 8:31, 33, 37). Satan may accuse us day and night, but he never wins a case!

Bound with Everlasting Chains

○∿

THE CONFINEMENT OF ANGELS

ROBABLY NO WRITER HAS MOLDED the popular view of hell more than Dante. Writing in the Middle Ages, Dante described his imaginary visits to hell, purgatory and heaven. He saw hell as a series of circles leading downward into the center of the earth. Each circle led to greater punishment for what Dante considered greater sins. The last circle, the ninth, was reserved for the cruelest of men and for Satan himself. In one of the areas on the ninth circle, men and women were consigned to a place not of fire and hot coals but of bitter frost and cold. The torment was unbearable.

The Bible does not give us an elaborate description of hell, but it does declare that such a place exists. We also find hints of special places of judgment within hell. These places are not reserved for evil human beings, however. They are reserved for sinful angels.

The demons who inhabit the heavens around us give us Christians the most trouble as we seek to walk in obedience to Christ. But there is another sizable group of demons who are not free to roam the earth. They are imprisoned by God.

When I speak on angels, the imprisonment of the angels always stirs a lot of interest among those who listen. I think that is because it's an aspect of the biblical teaching on angels that we don't hear much about. But I think the subject interests people for another, even more important reason. The fact that certain evil angels are imprisoned by God gives us a glimpse, a foreshadowing, of God's final victory over Satan and all his evil forces. We can be encouraged that even though the battle rages against us, the enemy is already in the process of being defeated.

I should say, too, that the Bible only gives us some small clues of what the confinement of the angels involves. I've tried to draw conclusions based on those clues, but we just can't be dogmatic on some of the issues I will address.

Permanent Confinement

The apostle Peter in his second letter talks extensively about God's power to punish those who are wicked and to rescue those who are righteous. To prove his point, Peter uses a series of examples, one of which involves angels: "God did not spare angels when they sinned, but sent them to hell, putting them into gloomy dungeons to be held for judgment" (2 Peter 2:4).

Peter tells us that there are some angels who, when they sinned, were laid hold of by God and cast into a prison. Peter describes this place vividly, calling it "gloomy dungeons" or "pits of darkness" (NASB). These angels are held in this horrible place by God until a time of judgment.

Peter refers to this place of confinement as hell—God "sent them to hell." That's what our English translations say, but the Greek word Peter uses is not the word *Hades*. Hades is the place where the spirits of unbelievers go immediately after death to await God's judgment (Luke 16:23, NIV note, NASB; Revelation 20:13). Peter is not talking about Hades. He uses the Greek word *Tartarus*. This is a special place. Perhaps it is a compartment of Hades, but it is a place of deep darkness, a horrible place of torment. The ancient world viewed Tartarus as a place deeper than hell itself, and the worst pit of gloom and darkness that existed anywhere.[1] God took this group of sinful angels and confined them there.

Second Peter 2:4 is the only place in the Bible where we find the word, *Tartarus*. But I think there is another reference to the angels' confinement in the tiny book of Jude:

And the angels who did not keep their positions of authority but abandoned their own home—these he has kept in darkness, bound with everlasting chains for judgment on the great Day. (Jude 6)

Not only are these angels in Tartarus, in pits of darkness, but they are bound there with everlasting chains.

Our response when we read these verses is, Who are these angels and what was their sin? They could *not* be the angels who first rebelled against God and followed Satan. That view has been suggested by some interpreters, but, if that were the case, all the fallen angels including Satan would today be confined. We know that is not true. Satan prowls around like a lion looking for his next victim (1 Peter 5:8).

It is my conviction that Peter and Jude are referring in these passages to some angels who sinned by coming to earth in human form and cohabiting with human women. The account is in Genesis 6:

When men began to increase in number on the earth and daughters were born to them, the sons of God saw that the daughters of men were beautiful, and they married any of them they chose. Then the LORD said, "My Spirit will not contend with man forever, for he is mortal; his days will be a hundred and twenty years."

The Nephilim were on the earth in those days—and also afterward—when the sons of God went to the daughters of men and had children by them. They were the heroes of old, men of renown.

The LORD saw how great man's wickedness on the earth had become, and that every inclination of the thoughts of his heart was only evil all the time. The LORD was grieved that he had made man on the earth, and his heart was filled with pain. So the LORD said, "I will wipe mankind, whom I have created, from the face of the earth—men and animals, and creatures that move along the ground, and birds of the air—for I am grieved that I have made them." But Noah found favor in the eyes of the LORD. (vv. 1-8)

Many students of the book of Genesis believe that "the sons of God" in this passage refers to godly human men. These men from the godly descendants of Seth (according to this view) married women from the ungodly line of Cain, "the daughters of men." This spiritual corruption led to moral decay and, eventually, to the judgment of the flood.[2]

I believe, however, along with other interpreters, that "the sons of God" were angels.[3] That particular phrase is used elsewhere in the Old Testament only of angels. In the book of Job (1:6; 2:1) the phrase includes all the angels, both holy and evil. Furthermore, the view that angels were the beings involved in this sin was the view held consistently by Jewish and Christian theologians until the fourth century a.d. As we will see, a large body of apocryphal literature was produced by Jewish writers based on this event recorded in Genesis 6.

If we accept the view that the sons of God were angels, however, several problems crop up. The biggest is, How can angels relate sexually to human women? It is possible that these angels possessed human men and fulfilled their lust through them. That does not explain, however, why their offspring were different from other human offspring. I believe that the angels directly cohabited with the human women and produced offspring called Nephilim—the word means "fallen ones"—who were half-human and half-angelic. It was that mixture of humankind and angelkind that produced such revulsion and pain in God's heart and prompted him to send the devastation of the flood.

A related problem is the sexuality of angels. Doesn't Jesus in Mark 12:25 say, "When the dead rise, they will neither marry nor be given in marriage; they will be like the angels in heaven"? Jesus does not say, however, that angels are sexless. He says that they do not reproduce among themselves. In fact, as we noted in the first chapter, angels are always described in Scripture as males. Furthermore, when angels appear to humans, they are often mistaken for human beings, and they function in very human ways. They can eat (Genesis 18:8); they can lead people by the hand (Genesis 19:16); they can speak human language (Luke 1:13); they can even appear enough like men to arouse the lust of the men of Sodom (Genesis 19:5). I am persuaded that angels can also function sexually as human males. At least they were allowed to do so before the flood.

This interpretation of Genesis 6 is confirmed by Jude in the New Testament. After describing the angels who abandoned their own home in verse 6, Jude links the sin of those angels with the sin of Sodom and Gomorrah:

> *In a similar way*, Sodom and Gomorrah and the surrounding towns gave themselves up to sexual immorality and perversion. They serve as an example of those who suffer the punishment of eternal fire. (v. 7)

A more literal translation of the Greek text makes the parallel even more evident:

> Also Sodom and Gomorrah and the cities around them, in a similar manner to these [angels], committing immorality and going away after different flesh, are set forth as a sign, undergoing punishment of eternal fire. (my translation)

The people of Sodom and Gomorrah were judged by God because they left their own domain sexually and went after strange or different (Greek *heteros*) flesh. The men of these cities abandoned the sexual order set down by God at creation and lusted after each other (see Romans 1:26-27). In the same way the angels of Genesis 6 left their proper abode (the realm of angels) and came into the realm of humanity to pursue different flesh. The angels desired a relationship that God never intended them to have.

The view that Genesis 6 involved angelic and human cohabitation was the consistent view of the Jews during the period of the Second Temple (200 b.c. to a.d. 100). The book of Enoch (*1 Enoch*), for example, contains a long description of the fall of the "watchers" (angels).⁴ Two hundred angels under the direction of two chief angels named Semjaza and Azazel descended to Mount Hermon and took human wives. Their offspring terrorized the earth. God sent the flood to destroy their children, and he bound the angels under the earth until the day of judgment. In the Septuagint, the Greek translation of the Hebrew Old Testament that was used widely by the Jews in the first century a.d., the phrase "sons of God" in Genesis 6 is rendered "angels of God."

Early church fathers also believed that Jude 6 referred to the angels in Genesis 6. It was not until the latter part of the fourth century a.d. that any other view was suggested.⁵ Eusebius, Justin, Athenagoras and Cyprian are just a few of the Christian fathers who accepted this position.

I'm not saying, of course, that we should believe all the legends that attached themselves to this event in Jewish and Christian literature. Genesis, Jude and 2 Peter are Scripture. The events the writers selected and included in these books we can rely upon as the truth.

Another question that this view raises is, *Why* did these angels intermingle with human beings? The immediate answer is that the sinful angels lusted for these beautiful human women. They were seeking some level of gratification from the relationship. On a deeper level, these angels were seeking to corrupt what God had created. Perhaps (and here I am entering the level of pure speculation) these angels were attempting to corrupt the human race by mingling humankind and angelkind in order to prevent the coming of the promised Redeemer who would crush the head of Satan (Genesis 3:15). They may have been trying to so infiltrate the human race that the Redeemer would be part angel and part human and would, therefore, provide redemption for angels as well as for humans. That possibility may be hinted at in Genesis 6:9, where Noah is described as a righteous man, "blameless among the people of his time." Literally translated that phrase means "perfect in his generations [or offspring]."

There was no corruption in Noah's line from the fallen angels. Noah's line survived the flood, while all other human lines ended.

One final issue I need to address is the offspring of this angel-human union— the Nephilim. Virtually every ancient culture has a mythology that includes stories of gods and goddesses coming to earth and relating sexually with human beings. The children of these unions are often the great heroes of that culture. In my opinion those myths grew out of a corrupted memory of this actual event in Genesis 6, when fallen angels invaded the realm of humanity and produced "the heroes of old, men of renown" (v. 4).

Continuing Confinement

Sinful angels can be confined even today in another place called the Abyss. In the previous chapter we looked at Mark's account of Jesus' encounter with the demon-possessed man in the region of the Gerasenes. Luke includes a reference to the abyss in his version of the account:

> Jesus asked him [the evil spirit], "what is your name?"
>
> "Legion," he replied, because many demons had gone into him. And they begged him repeatedly not to order them to go into the Abyss. (8:30-31)

Apparently at God's discretion demons still can be confined to this "Abyss." No demon wants to go there. It is obviously a place of torment for them, because earlier in Luke's account the demon said to Jesus, "I beg you, don't torture me!" (8:28). In Matthew's Gospel the demons say, "Have you come here to torture us before the appointed time?" (8:29). These demons even knew God's timetable for their confinement and destruction!

According to John's record in the book of Revelation, the Abyss will be opened in the future. As seven angels sound their trumpets in heaven, waves of judgment will sweep over the earth. As the fifth trumpet sounds, another angel opens the Abyss (Revelation 9:1). Smoke billows out and, from the smoke, beings like locusts swarm over the earth. What appear as locusts are most likely demons who have been confined in the Abyss but who now are set free to torment humanity. The creatures have "as king over them the angel of the Abyss, whose name in Hebrew is Abaddon, and in Greek, Apollyon" (Revelation 9:11).

Future Confinement

All the fallen angels, including Satan, will be confined in the Abyss during the time of Christ's reign on earth. John relates the event:

> And I saw an angel coming down out of heaven, having the key to the Abyss and holding in his hand a great chain. He seized the dragon, that ancient serpent, who is the devil, or Satan, and bound him for a thousand years. He threw him into the Abyss, and locked and sealed it over him, to keep him from deceiving the nations anymore until the thousand years were ended. After that, he must be set free for a short time. (Revelation 20:1-3)

At the end of Christ's reign, Satan and his angels are released for a time:

> When the thousand years are over, Satan will be released from his prison and will go out to deceive the nations in the four corners of the earth—Gog and Magog— to gather them for battle. (Revelation 20:7-8)

Final Confinement

The day will come, however, when Satan and all his angels will be confined forever in the lake of fire. The old enemy of God and God's people will bow to Christ and will confess that Jesus is Lord (Philippians 2:10-11). Then God will kick him into absolute darkness forever.

The devil, who deceived them, was thrown into the lake of burning sulfur....[He] will be tormented day and night for ever and ever. (Revelation 20:10)

Satan, along with all the angels who followed him and all the human beings who rejected God's gracious salvation, "will be tormented with burning sulfur *in the presence of the holy angels* and of the Lamb" (Revelation 14:10). The lake of fire, eternal hell, was created and prepared by God as a place of eternal confinement and judgment for the devil and his angels (Matthew 25:41).

In a day when it often seems that evil and violence have gained the upper hand in our society, Christians can know that God's ultimate victory is sure. Satan's reign will give way to God's reign. God is so certain of that final victory, secured through Christ's redemptive sacrifice, that he can record Satan's conquest in terms of an accomplished fact.

CHAPTER NINE

An Angel Strengthened Him

∽

JESUS AND ANGELS

KNOW A MAN PERSONALLY who has had more encounters with angels than anyone in history. In the course of his lifetime, angels both good and evil have appeared to him many times. He has conversed with angels, argued with them, silenced a few and claimed on one occasion to have several thousand at his disposal. He knows more about angels than any other human being—not because he has read all the books on angels but because he created them! The man's name, of course, is Jesus.

In an earlier chapter I made a point that I need to reemphasize in this context: Jesus is the Creator, Lord and Sustainer of the angels. Paul in Colossians 1:15-17 says:

> He is the image of the invisible God, the firstborn over all creation. For by him all things were created: things in heaven and on earth, visible and invisible, whether thrones or powers or rulers or authorities; all things were created by him and for him. He is before all things, and in him all things hold together.

Jesus not only brought all the angels into existence. He also sustains those angels by his power, just as he sustains us and just as he holds the entire universe together.

Since we are centuries removed from the birth of Christianity, we usually don't question Jesus' superiority over the angels, but many Jews of the first century highly revered angels. Knowing this, the writer of the letter to Hebrew Christians spends several opening paragraphs emphasizing the fact that Jesus is far more exalted than any angel. He notes that God actually commands the angels to worship Jesus: "And again, when God brings his firstborn into the world, he says, 'Let all God's angels worship him'" (Hebrews 1:6).

Before Jesus became a man, the angels worshiped him as their Creator. And when God brought Jesus into the world as a man, the angels were commanded to worship and adore him no less. Even in human flesh as a tiny baby, Jesus was the sovereign Lord, God the Son.

God's command and Jesus' position as Creator make the next fact about Jesus' relationship to the angels almost unbelievable. When Jesus became human, he was made *lower* than the angels for a time. The writer of Hebrews speaks again:

> It is not to angels that he has subjected the world to come, about which we are speaking. But there is a place where someone has testified:
> "What is man that you are mindful of him,
>   the son of man that you care for him?
> You made him a little lower than the angels [or, "You made him for a little while lower than the angels"; NIV margin];
>   you crowned him with glory and honor
>   and put everything under his feet."
> In putting everything under him, God left nothing that is not subject to him. Yet at present we do not see everything subject to him. But we see Jesus, who was made a little lower than the angels, now crowned with glory and honor because he suffered death, so that by the grace of God he might taste death for everyone. (Hebrews 2:5-9)

What a wonderful blessing it is to be a human being! We were created to be crowned with glory and honor. Unfortunately, that hasn't happened yet. At the present time not all things are subject to us. Right now we are lower than the angels in terms of glory and honor. God is at the top of the "glory" scale, angels are next, and somewhere below them comes humanity.

A friend of mine was the leader of an engineering division within one of the Big Three automakers. Because of restructuring, he found himself in a different unit at the bottom of the engineering ladder. It takes a lot of humility to handle a change like that gracefully.

Jesus was in the "deity range" on the scale of glory. But in order to identify with us and in order to redeem us, Jesus became fully human. He didn't come to earth as an angel or as a glorified human being. (Sorry—Jesus had no halo!) He came as a mortal human just like us. In the realm of his humanity, Jesus was made lower than the angels for a little while. He didn't cease to be God, but he identified fully with us in his humanity.

I do not think that you and I have begun to grasp the price Jesus paid just to become human. He paid the price of our sin on the cross, and that was a wonderful gift. But he paid a great price just in humbling himself to become a man, and he did it all willingly, voluntarily. For the sheer joy of seeing us brought to glory with him, the Lord and Creator of the angels lived for thirty-three years as a man, lower than the very beings he had created.

We also know that eventually Jesus was exalted above the angels once again:

> The Son is the radiance of God's glory and the exact representation of his being, sustaining all things by his powerful word. After he had provided purification for sins, he sat down at the right hand of the Majesty in heaven. So he became as much superior to the angels as the name he has inherited is superior to theirs. (Hebrews 1:3-4)

Jesus died on the cross, and three days later he rose from the dead. Forty days later he ascended into heaven, where he sat down at the Father's right hand. In his humanity Jesus was exalted above the angels. As the God-man, not just as God but as the eternal God-man, Jesus was elevated to the place above the angels that we will occupy some day as redeemed, glorified human beings.

Because Jesus had such intimate contact with angels before and after his ministry, we would expect that during his earthly ministry angels would be actively involved with everything he did. As we survey the Gospel records, that is exactly what we find.

Joyous Hosts at His Birth

The gospel story begins with two miraculous births, and the angel who announced them both was Gabriel, "an angel of the Lord." He was sent to Zechariah, a priest in Israel, to tell him that he and his wife (who was barren) would produce a marvelous son. Their son, John, would be the forerunner of the promised Messiah (Luke 1:11-20). Six months later Gabriel was sent to a virgin woman named Mary who lived in Nazareth. He told her that she would conceive a child miraculously and bear a son who would be the Son of the Most High (Luke 1:26-38). A short time after that an angel (perhaps Gabriel again) appeared to Joseph in a dream to assure him that Mary had not been unfaithful to him and that the child conceived in her was of the Holy Spirit (Matthew 1:20-23).

When the time came, an angel of the Lord appeared to shepherds outside Bethlehem to announce Jesus' birth to them. As they heard the joyous news, the shepherds saw a multitude of the heavenly host join that one angel in praising God (Luke 2:9-14). After the birth Joseph again saw an angel in a dream. This time the angel warned him to flee to Egypt to escape Herod's murderous plot to kill Jesus. After Herod's death, the angel came yet again to Joseph in a dream and told him to return to Galilee (Matthew 2:13-20).

Strengthening Agents During His Ministry

The next recorded encounter Jesus had with angels came almost thirty years later, when the Spirit led him into the wilderness to be tempted by an evil angel, the devil himself (Matthew 4:1; Luke 4:1-2). Three times Satan came to Jesus, and each time Jesus rebuked him. After the temptation holy angels came and ministered to Jesus (Matthew 4:11; Mark 1:13).

Angels exercised a protective ministry over Jesus throughout his life. During Satan's attempt to disqualify Jesus as the Son of God, Satan took him to the pinnacle of the temple and challenged Jesus to throw himself down. Satan even quoted Psalm 91:11-12, Scripture that assured Jesus' safety:

> He [God] will command his angels concerning you, and they will lift you up in their hands, so that you will not strike your foot against a stone. (Matthew 4:6)

Jesus responded not by doubting God's promise but by pointing out also from Scripture (Deuteronomy 6:16) the stupidity of putting God and his Word to the test just because the devil dares you to do it.

A statement Jesus made in the garden of Gethsemane gives us some idea of the extent of the angels' protective ministry over Jesus. When the crowd came to arrest Jesus, Peter took out a sword, swung it over his head like a fishing pole and cut off the ear of the high priest's slave. Jesus rebuked Peter with this:

> Put your sword back in its place....Do you think I cannot call on my Father, and he will at once put at my disposal more than twelve legions of angels? But how then would the Scriptures be fulfilled that say it must happen this way? (Matthew 26:52-54)

A Roman legion was six thousand men. Jesus said that at his word more than 72,000 angels would come instantly to his aid. That's a lot of firepower! Jesus had abundant angelic protection at his disposal, but he never called them. If he had called them that night, God's Word promising human redemption never would have been fulfilled.

As Jesus prayed in the garden earlier that evening, he had talked to one of those angels. Luke tells us that an angel from heaven appeared to Jesus, strengthening him for the ordeal ahead (Luke 22:43). But through the humiliation of his arrest and the agony of the cross, no angel came to Jesus' aid. He bore the full fury of God's wrath all alone. He drank the cup that the Father gave him to the bitter dregs.

Demonic Forces During His Ministry

While holy angels ministered to Jesus, evil angels were arrayed in force against him. We've already noted the confrontation between Jesus and Satan in the wilderness, but Satan's work as Jesus' adversary didn't end there. Twice we are told that Satan entered into Judas the betrayer (Luke 22:3; John 13:27). Jesus even saw Satan's hand behind Simon Peter's suggestion that Jesus should avoid his approaching death (Matthew 16:23; Mark 8:33). "Get behind me, Satan!" Jesus said. "You are a stumbling block to me." He knew that Satan would try to get Peter's faith to fail, and he prayed to keep that from happening (Luke 22:31-32). Jesus also knew that Satan's final defeat was certain. In the initial ministry of the seventy-two disciples, Jesus saw a foreshadowing of Satan's conquest—"I saw Satan fall like lightning from heaven" (Luke 10:18). And even with the cross ahead of him, Jesus declared that "the prince of this world now stands condemned" (John 16:11).

One of the most serious charges leveled against Jesus by his human enemies was that his miracles were performed by Satan's power. The reality of Jesus' miracles was not questioned, only their source. People accused, "It is only by Beelzebub, the prince of demons, that this fellow drives out demons." Jesus responded, "If Satan drives out Satan, he is divided against himself. How then can his kingdom stand?" (Matthew 12:24, 26). Then Jesus clearly stated his source of power: "But if I drive out demons by the Spirit of God, then the kingdom of God has come upon you" (v. 28). Knowing that the Pharisees disbelieved his claim, Jesus warned that blasphemy against the Holy Spirit is an unforgivable sin (v. 32).

Satan's angels also play a dramatic part in Jesus' ministry. The Gospels are filled with accounts of the conflict between Jesus and demons. Jesus and the New Testament writers saw no difference between a demon's activity and Satan's activity. Luke, the physician, records Jesus' healing of a woman "who had been crippled *by a spirit* for eighteen years" (13:11). When the synagogue ruler rebuked Jesus for healing on the Sabbath day, Jesus shot back,

> You hypocrites! Doesn't each of you on the Sabbath untie his ox or donkey from the stall and lead it out to give it water? Then should not this woman, a daughter of Abraham, *whom Satan has kept bound* for eighteen long years, be set free on the Sabbath day from what bound her? (13:15-16, italics mine)

Jesus and his disciples encountered various "unclean" or "wicked" spirits who were under Satan's power (Mark 1:23, NIV note; Matthew 12:45). Many times the Gospel writers describe demons by the effects they produce. Matthew describes a "demon-possessed man who was blind and mute" (Matthew 12:22). We read of a boy "possessed by a spirit that has robbed him of speech" (Mark 9:17). Mark ascribes the uncontrolled violence and extreme strength of the Gerasene man to the "legion" of demons that possessed him (Mark 5:1-5, 9). Most of modern psychology may reject demonic influence as superstition, but Jesus and his apostles had no trouble attributing some physical sicknesses or emotional oppression directly to demonic activity.

Perhaps the most startling aspect of Jesus' confrontations with demonic forces was the way they immediately recognized his position and power. Mark says that Jesus would not allow demons to speak "because they knew who he was" (Mark 1:34). The demons in the Gerasene man recognized Jesus even "from a distance."

76

The man ran to Jesus and knelt, screaming, "What do you want with me, Jesus, Son of the Most High God?" (Mark 5:7). In another encounter early in his ministry, Jesus came face to face in a synagogue with a man possessed by a demon, who said, "I know who you are—the Holy One of God!" (Luke 4:33-34). Jesus shouted, "Be quiet!" What the demons said about Jesus was true, but Jesus told them to be quiet because he didn't want unsolicited testimonials from demons.

Jesus said that one crucial aspect of his messianic ministry was to set captives free (Luke 4:18). He certainly accomplished that by freeing people held in the grip of evil angelic forces. The demons had no alternative but to yield to Christ's superior power. Jesus extended this power by giving his followers authority over demons. He first sent out the twelve to preach and to work miracles, including healing the demon-possessed (Luke 9:1). Then he sent out the seventy-two to do the same; they returned from their mission, rejoicing that even the demons were subject to them (Luke 10:17). The name of Jesus had the power to overcome any wicked foe.

And Jesus' name still has that power! An elder in the church I pastor spent his B.C. (before Christ) years in the grip of drugs and the immoral lifestyle so prevalent in our culture. Then one day he heard the gospel and believed in Christ. Some faithful believers followed their evangelistic ministry with a ministry of deliverance as they rebuked the demons who were actively oppressing this man. Through a direct battle with the forces of evil, these folks called on the Lord Jesus to set this captive free. Just as in the days of the New Testament, Jesus' name and authority prevailed.

Heralds at His Resurrection

On the first day of the week after Jesus' death and burial, angels went to his tomb with a message. When a group of women, who planned to anoint the body with spices, drew near, there was a violent earthquake, for an angel of the Lord came down from heaven and, going to the tomb, rolled back the stone and sat on it. His appearance was like lightning, and his clothes were white as snow. The guards [at the tomb] were so afraid of him that they shook and became like dead men. (Matthew 28:2-4)

The same angel addressed the women and told them that Jesus had risen from the dead (vv. 5-7). In Mark's account the angel is described as "a young man dressed in a white robe" (Mark 16:5). Luke's more detailed report says that the women saw "two men in clothes that gleamed like lightning" (Luke 24.4). The two men Jesus met on the road to Emmaus later that resurrection day confirmed that the women reported seeing more than one angel at the empty tomb—they saw "a vision of *angels*" (Luke 24:23). John and Peter, two of Jesus' followers, came to the tomb shortly after the women, but they did not encounter any angels (John 20:3-9). Mary Magdalene then returned in sorrow and unbelief to the tomb. She bent down to peer into the tomb and saw "two angels in white, seated where Jesus' body had been, one at the head and the other at the foot" (John 20:10-12).

Warriors at His Return

When Jesus ascended into heaven forty days later, "two men dressed in white" stood by the disciples, who were gazing up into heaven. The angels said, "Why do you stand here looking into the sky? This same Jesus—will come back" (Acts 1:10-11). When he returns, angels will play a prominent role in the events surrounding his coming.

At the rapture of the church, those of us who are "in Christ" will hear a shout and the voice of the archangel (1 Thessalonians 4:16). We aren't told what the archangel will say, but maybe he will say what an angel said to the apostle John in Revelation 4:1, "Come up here!"

When Christ returns to earth in his glory to destroy his enemies and the enemies of his people, angels will come with him. Paul in 2 Thessalonians 1:7 says, "The Lord Jesus [will be] revealed from heaven in blazing fire with his powerful angels." The book of Revelation, which unfolds the details of Christ's return, uses the word *angel* sixty-one times—the most of any New Testament book.

When he was on earth, Jesus knew what angels would do at his return (Mark 8:38). He told a series of parables one day and then interpreted them for his disciples. In the parable of the field sown with both good seed and bad, Jesus said:

> The one who sowed the good seed is the Son of Man. The field is the world, and the good seed stands for the sons of the kingdom. The weeds are the sons of the evil one, and the enemy who sows them is the devil. The harvest is the end of the age, and the harvesters are angels.
>
> As the weeds are pulled up and burned in the fire, so it will be at the end of the age. The Son of Man will send out his angels, and they will weed out of his kingdom everything that causes sin and all who do evil. They will throw them into the fiery furnace, where there will be weeping and gnashing of teeth. (Matthew 13:37-42)

The parable of the net full of all kinds of fish imparts the same truth. When the fishermen pulled the net to shore, they sorted the fish. Jesus explained the meaning of the parable like this:

> This is how it will be at the end of the age. The angels will come and separate the wicked from the righteous and throw them into the fiery furnace, where there will be weeping and gnashing of teeth. (Matthew 13:49-50)

Angels will not only separate out the wicked and unbelieving when Jesus returns, but also gather God's believing remnant, the elect, into the joys of Christ's kingdom.

And he [the Son of Man] will send his angels with a loud trumpet call, and they will gather his elect from the four winds, from one end of the heavens to the other. (Matthew 24:31; see also Mark 13:27)

Jesus and the Angel of the Lord

A remarkable being punctuates the pages of the Old Testament on several occasions. At critical times in the history of God's people, key individuals were visited by a powerful and wonderful person—the angel of the Lord. As we read the accounts of the appearances of the angel of the Lord, however, we are forced to conclude that this being was more than just a normal angel of God.

Two facts become clear from a study of the biblical text. First, this angel is identified as "the Lord" or even as "God." Second, though the angel is identified as the Lord, he is also distinguished from another person called "the Lord"—an implication at least of plural persons within the being of God.[1]

One of the best-known appearances of the angel of the Lord recorded in Scripture is his encounter with Moses on Mount Horeb.

Now Moses was tending the flock of Jethro his father-in-law, the priest of Midian, and he led the flock to the far side of the desert and came to Horeb, the mountain of God. There the angel of the LORD appeared to him in flames of fire from within a bush. (Exodus 3:1-2)

This angel made an astonishing claim: "I am the God of your father, the God of Abraham, the God of Isaac and the God of Jacob." Moses' response was to hide his face, "because he was afraid to look at God" (v. 6).

When the angel of the Lord appeared to Manoah's wife in the days of the judges, he told her that she would bear a son. When she in turn told her husband about the encounter, she said, "A man of God came to me. He looked like an angel of God, very awesome." Manoah prayed and asked God to send the man again. When the angel came again and then departed in the flame of the sacrificial fire, Manoah realized that the man had been the angel of the Lord. He exclaimed, "We are doomed to die....We have seen God!" (Judges 13:1-22).

Abraham encountered this same divine being. As he drew back the knife to kill his son, Isaac, as a sacrifice, "the angel of the Lord called out" and told Abraham not to harm the boy. The angel added, "Now I know that you fear God, because you have not withheld from me your son" (Genesis 22:12).

The visions of the prophet Zechariah show most clearly the distinction between the angel of the Lord and another referred to as "the Lord." Acting as an intercessor for the people of Judah, the angel of the Lord addresses "the Lord Almighty" and asks for mercy on Judah (Zechariah 1:11-12). In a later vision Zechariah sees the angel of the Lord defending Israel's high priest, Joshua, against the accusations of Satan in the presence of the Lord (Zechariah 3:1-2).

These observations about the angel of the Lord have led most biblical scholars to conclude that "the angel of the Lord" in the Old Testament was a reincarnate manifestation of the Lord Jesus. He was called an angel because he functioned as the Father's messenger, but he is clearly deity himself. Furthermore, when we come to the New Testament, we encounter "*an* angel of the Lord" several times (Matthew 1:20; Acts 8:26; 12:7) but never "*the* angel of the Lord."

For a number of months I visited a dear woman of God who was slowly dying. Often when we were alone in her hospital room, Berneice would say, "Read the psalm you always read. I love the 'angel part.'" When she died, I read Psalm 34 at her funeral: "The angel of the LORD encamps around those who fear him, and he delivers them" (v. 7). That is certainly true of the Lord Jesus for those who know him personally by faith. His presence surrounds us; his power sustains us; his protection secures us against any foe.

He Will Send Forth His Angels

∽

ANGELS AND HUMANS

WOMAN WAS IN THE CRITICAL CARE UNIT with a raging infection. She was not expected to survive. I was her pastor at the time, and as I stood by her bedside and talked to her, she would respond only with nods or whispers. Finally she said, "Who is the man standing in the corner, dressed in white? He's been standing there all night and all day today." When I looked at the corner of the room, no one was there. I said, "What does he look like?" "Can't you see him?" she replied. "He's all in white, and he is so strong. It's like he is standing guard. I'm almost afraid to speak in his presence."

I asked the nurse when I left the room if the patient had said anything about a man in her room. The nurse reassured me that the woman was just hallucinating. "Has she seen anything else that wasn't there?" I asked. "Oh, no, she is very perceptive—except for the man in white!" As I walked out of the hospital I was convinced that what this dear child of God saw in her room was not a hallucination. It was a very real angel of God.

Virtually every time holy angels show themselves to humans beings—in biblical accounts or even today—the humans react with awe and alarm. Though captivated by the angels' majesty, we are frightened by their manner. Most often in Scripture angels immediately reassure people: "Do not be afraid" (Luke 1:13, 30; 2:10). The angels of God do not come to terrorize his people but to bring "good news of great joy."

A Comparison of Glory

Our initial response to these glorious beings does point out, however, a key difference between angels and human beings: human beings are lower than angels in terms of greatness and glory. While I discussed this briefly in the previous chapter in relation to Jesus' humanity, we need to be reminded that as humans all of us are less glorious and less powerful than angels. The writer of Hebrews makes that point very clearly:

It is not to angels that he has subjected the world to come, about which we are speaking. But there is a place where someone has testified:

"What is man that you are mindful of him,
    the son of man that you care for him?
You made him a little lower than the angels;
    you crowned him with glory and honor
    and put everything under his feet." (Hebrews 2:5-8)

The phrase "a little lower than the angels" can also be translated, "you made him [man] *for a little while* lower than the angels" (see, for example, the NASB translation).

If that is the correct translation, the implication is that humankind will not always be lower than the angels. In our present state we are lower; in the future, glorified state of believers that relationship will be reversed. When our redemption is complete and our bodies are glorified, we will not be like angels. We will be like Christ (1 Corinthians 15:49; 1 John 3:2). God will exalt us above the angels.

The apostle Paul amplified that concept when he declared that believers will someday sit in judgment over the angels. The Corinthian Christians were dragging fellow believers into secular courts before unbelieving judges to settle disputes. Paul rebuked them and instructed them to settle their differences before godly men and women of the church. After all, he argued, believers will one day judge the world—and the angels: "Do you not know that the saints will judge the world?...Do you not know that we will judge angels?" (1 Corinthians 6:2-3). Paul is most likely referring to fallen angels. At the final judgment we will have some part in judging the very angels who attack us now.

The Worship of Angels

Since God's angels are above us in position, strength, wisdom and beauty, we might be tempted to think more highly of them than we should. We are to respect their power and authority as God's messengers and even as Satan's cohorts, but we are never to revere or worship them.

This was a real problem in the early church. Certain groups of Jews held angels in very high regard. An early Christian heresy called Gnosticism advocated worshiping and praying to angels as intermediaries between God and men. The apostle Paul attacked that teaching in Colossians 2:18, saying, "Do not let anyone who delights in false humility and *the worship of angels* disqualify you for the prize" (italics mine).

The apostle John was so overwhelmed by his vision of the new Jerusalem that he fell down at the feet of his angel guide to worship him. The angel's response was immediate: "Do not do it! I am a fellow servant with you and with your brothers the prophets and of all who keep the words of this book. Worship God!" (Revelation 22:9). The Bible makes it unmistakably clear that we must never worship an angel or any creature of God. God alone deserves our worship. In spite of the fact that angels are exalted above us, they are still just creatures of God, subjects in God's kingdom like we are.

I want to emphasize that point because in our culture we are seeing a growing influence of pagan religions, in which ancient gods and goddesses are worshiped. The reverence of ancient spirits or false gods or primitive warriors who speak through spirit channels is nothing more than the worship of fallen angels—demons. "The sacrifices [acts of worship] of pagans are offered to demons, not to God" (1 Corinthians 10:20; see also Deuteronomy 32:17; Revelation 9:20).

We as believers need to keep ourselves untouched by this kind of demonic power. If you traffic in anything that smacks of the occult or New Age mysticism or spirit channeling, you are flirting with dangerous demonic realms. I think that applies to the movies and the television programs we watch. It applies to the novels we read. Perverted entertainment focused on demons and Satan does nothing but open our minds to demonic suggestion and our hearts to demonic oppression.

A young college student came to see me a few years ago. She was a Christian, but she had become consumed with a fear of demons. As we talked I soon discovered that for several months she had been watching videotapes of horror movies in which demons or Satan played a part. She had focused so much on the power of these evil forces that she had begun to magnify them even above God. She had also neglected her own time in the Word and participation in church and campus-ministry activities.

After our conversation this young woman took a direct course of action. She went home and smashed her collection of horror tapes—a drastic course of action that Jesus recommends in serious situations (Matthew 5:29-30). She then found two older women who would pray with her regularly. Her spiritual life soon regained its balance.

Extreme fascination with any aspect of the satanic realm—astrology, New Age paganism, witchcraft, the occult—can lead you down paths of spiritual deception and oppression. The Scriptures counsel us in a different direction. "Whatever is true, whatever is noble, whatever is right, whatever is pure, whatever is lovely, whatever is admirable—if anything is excellent or praiseworthy—think about such things" (Philippians 4:8).

Agents of God's Judgment

The final aspect of the relationship between angels and human beings that I want to explore is the work of angels toward the world. Men and women who reject Christ and who seek to persecute believers occasionally may encounter angels—but they are angels of judgment.

Two cities in Herod Agrippa's realm were locked in a dispute with their king (probably over taxes!). In an attempt to bring the people of Tyre and Sidon under control, Herod cut off their food supply. In desperation the leaders of those cities asked for an audience with Herod to make peace. When Herod mounted his throne and made a speech, the defeated city leaders, trying to gain Herod's favor, shouted, "This is the voice of a god, not of a man." Herod accepted their praise and paid a huge price for his pride. "Immediately, because Herod did not give praise to God, an angel of the Lord struck him down, and he was eaten by worms and died" (Acts 12:20-23). God dispatched an angel to execute swift judgment on one ungodly, arrogant man.

Two angels came to Lot and his family and told them to flee from Sodom because God had sent *them* to destroy it. "*We* are going to destroy this place....[The LORD] has sent *us* to destroy it" (Genesis 19:13). The angels were powerless to begin until Lot and his family were safely beyond the area marked out for destruction (v. 22). As the record of Sodom's destruction continues, we see the harmony between God and his angels. Even though the angels did the work, we are told that "*the LORD* rained down burning sulfur....God destroyed the cities of the plain" (vv. 24, 29).

When God pours out his final wrath on sinful humanity, angels play a prominent role as dispensers of God's judgment (Revelation 8:2; 15:1; 18:1). God's holy angels may even play a part in guarding the eternal lake of fire (Revelation 14:10).

In the Council of His Holy Ones

GOD, ANGELS AND SALVATION

LITTLE BOY CAME UP TO ME after I had given a message on angels, and he asked a very probing question—"Why does God need angels?" If God is all-powerful and all-knowing, why all these millions of angels to do his work? Don't they just get in God's way?

One young girl in Sunday school was sure she had figured out the celestial arrangements. "Angels," she said, "keep God's house clean."

God, of course, does not *need* anyone or anything. He did not create us because he was lonely, and he did not create angels to keep his house clean. God is the all-sufficient and self-sufficient One. We are dependent creatures; God is totally free. That does *not* mean, however, that God created angels (or us) on a whim. He is a God of purpose. Having decided to make a kingdom to rule as Sovereign, he also chose to create two kinds of personal beings to serve him in that kingdom—human beings and angelic beings. Not wanting servants who would mindlessly worship him, God granted both groups the power of choice. He gave them a will, the ability to choose to obey him or to choose not to obey him.

Adam and Eve exercised their will and disobeyed God's clear command. They became, in that moment, sinners before him. Furthermore, to their offspring they passed on the legacy of a fallen, sinful human nature. Yet God's great grace allows individuals to once again choose obedience. God himself became a human being, Jesus, and paid the penalty of human sin by dying on the cross.

With the way now cleared to a reconciliation with God, all those who believe in the Lord Jesus receive forgiveness (Ephesians 1:7-8; 2:8-9, 13).

Choosing Once and for All

God also gave angels the power of choice; some of them chose to obey and some to rebel. Holy angels don't need salvation, because they have obeyed God perfectly throughout their existence. But fallen angels are destined (as all of us were) for an eternity in hell. What about them? Isn't there some provision in God's plan of redemption for them? The answer is no! The Bible clearly teaches that there is no redemption for fallen angels. Once an angel willfully sins, that angel is confirmed in his evil forever.

Whoever wrote the book of Hebrews had thought deeply about the subject of angels and salvation. Several times the writer emphasizes the fact that salvation does not extend to angels. In Hebrews 1:14 he says, "Are not all angels ministering spirits sent to serve those who will inherit salvation?" We can infer from this verse that angels are in a different category from those who will inherit salvation. God's angels minister to those humans who are recipients of salvation. They do not minister to lost angels.

Nor does Christ's salvation work apply to sinful angels, says the writer in the next chapter:

> Since the children have flesh and blood, he too shared in their humanity so that by his death he might destroy him who holds the power of death—that is, the devil— and free those who all their lives were held in slavery by their fear of death. For surely it is not angels he helps, but Abraham's descendants. (Hebrews 2:14-16)

His argument is very straightforward. Jesus became fully human so that he could die as our substitute on the cross. Because Jesus died in our place, he can provide help (that is, salvation help) to us. Jesus does not, however, provide that help to angels. He did not come as an angel. He did not become the God-angel. Jesus did not pay the price for angelic sin. He paid the price for human sin.

Nowhere in Scripture does God describe an atoning work for angels. No sacrificial system foreshadowed it; no redemption is ever offered to angels. The only result that came from the cross for fallen angels was their defeat and the assurance of their condemnation (Colossians 2:15).

The apostle Peter had explored the wonders of God's salvation. At one point he states clearly, "God *did not spare* angels when they sinned, but sent them to hell [Tartarus]" (2 Peter 2:4). He also realized that the angels were merely curious onlookers to redemption.

> Concerning this salvation, the prophets, who spoke of the grace that was to come to you, searched intently and with the greatest care, trying to find out the time and circumstances to which the Spirit of Christ in them was pointing when he predicted the sufferings of Christ and the glories that would follow. It was revealed to them that they were not serving themselves but you, when they spoke of the things that have now been told you by those who have preached the gospel to you by the Holy Spirit sent from heaven. Even angels long to look into these things. (1 Peter 1:10-12)

Angels are intrigued by God's whole redemptive program. We who are Christians have received the salvation that God promised throughout the Old Testament. But angels have never experienced personally this salvation. They long to understand it, but they can never enter into it fully. The only way angels can learn about God's grace in salvation is by watching how God saves fallen human beings.[1]

We might well ask, Why does God provide salvation for fallen, rebellious human beings but not for fallen, rebellious angelic beings? We are both God's creatures. We as human beings certainly do not *deserve* God's grace more than the angels do. *We* have rebelled against God. *We* have gone our own way. Why does God make this distinction?

The only answer we have is that it was God's own choice to do so. God doesn't tell us why, and he is not obligated to tell us why. Our response should not be to question God but to bow before him and to thank him that in his grace he saved us.

Once Satan and each angel who followed him in rebellion made the choice to set their wills against God, they were locked into that choice forever. We aren't told if the angels knew that would happen, but they can never change their lost condition. That is *not* true of us as human beings. As long as we are alive, we always have the opportunity to believe in Christ. Once we die, our eternity is sealed either as a redeemed child of God or as a doomed human being. If you have never received Jesus Christ, the Son of God, as your Savior, I would invite you—no, I would plead with you—to believe in him. In spite of our rebellion, God loves us and has provided a Savior to pay the penalty that we deserve. Christ will forgive you and save you if you turn to him in genuine faith.

Ministering to God

Even though God chose not to provide redemption for angels, he did create them with a purpose in his eternal plan. Some of the most important and amazing ministries angels have are ministries directed toward God himself.

Primarily, the angels worship and adore God by praising his character and his works (just as *we* worship God). But they don't worship by sitting with downcast eyes and folded wings listening to quiet organ music. They shout with joy. They sing God's praises. They proclaim in loud, thunderous voices the majesty and glory of God. Angelic seraphim call to one another above God's throne, "Holy, holy, holy is the LORD Almighty" (Isaiah 6:3; see also Revelation 4:8). In Revelation 5 John records that all the angelic hosts worship the Lamb, God the Son. The angels never stop giving praise and honor to God.

Angels also stand ready to obey God's commands. They are his servants.

Praise the LORD, you his angels,
  you mighty ones who do his bidding,
  who obey his word.
Praise the LORD, all his heavenly hosts,
  you his servants who do his will. (Psalm 103:20-21)

The angels stand in God's presence waiting to respond to his will and word. Sometimes the angels act as messengers to communicate the will of God to certain chosen human beings. At other times God sends them to administer his judgment or chastening (against a city, Sodom, Genesis 19:13; against David, God's chosen leader of Israel, 1 Chronicles 21:8-15; and against King Herod Agrippa, Acts 12:23).

Angels work as fellow tenants with believers and with the church as a whole in advancing and expanding the kingdom of God (Revelation 22:8-9). That aspect of the ministry of angels may explain one of the most mysterious references to angels in the Bible. When the early church deacon Stephen was dragged before the Sanhedrin for questioning, they note his startling appearance: "All who were sitting in the Sanhedrin looked intently at Stephen, and they saw that his face was like the face of an angel" (Acts 6:15). What does an angel's face look like? Perhaps they saw the face of a person fully submissive to the Lord Jesus and perfectly calm in the heat of opposition—a faithful tenant of a faithful Master.

Aiding Scripture Writers

Writing the Scriptures was no easy task, especially for the prophets, so angels often acted as God's agents in interpreting their prophetic visions. Angels instructed and offered insight to Daniel (Daniel 8:17-19; 9:21-22) as well as to Zechariah (Zechariah 1:14-17; 4:1-6) and Ezekiel (Ezekiel 40:3-4). An angel even gave the apostle John a guided tour of heaven (Revelation 21:9-10). Fortunately we have John's record of this remarkable tour, because that same angel told him not to keep secret these "trustworthy and true" words of prophecy (Revelation 22:10).

Perhaps the most striking example of this particular ministry occurred at Mount Sinai, where God gave Moses the Ten Commandments and additional laws relating to Israel's obedience to God. Though never explicitly mentioned in the Old Testament, Moses hinted that the angels were involved in this long process. In his final blessing on Israel, Moses says,

> The LORD came from Sinai and dawned over them from Seir; he shone forth from Mount Paran. He came with myriads of holy ones from the south, from his mountain slopes. (Deuteronomy 33:2)

Many Jews in the first century a.d. believed that Moses received the law through angels. Stephen, a wise man "full of God's grace and power," states it as a fact (Acts 6:8-10). As Stephen defends himself before the same Jewish council that had condemned Jesus, he takes them through the history of Israel, demonstrating how the people had habitually disobeyed the Lord. He says,

> Was there ever a prophet your fathers did not persecute? They even killed those who predicted the coming of the Righteous One. And now you have betrayed and murdered him—you who have received the law that was put into effect through angels but have not obeyed it. (Acts 7:52-53)

According to Stephen, the law "was put into effect through angels." Earlier in his speech Stephen had described Moses' experience on Sinai:

> He was in the assembly in the desert, *with the angel who spoke to him on Mount Sinai,* and with our fathers; and he received living words to pass on to us. (Acts 7:38)

The apostle Paul confirms in Galatians 3:19 that "the law was put into effect through angels." The word of angels in bringing the law to Moses did not diminish the law's authority, of course. It was still the Word of God, and Israel was responsible to hear it and obey.

It was the agency of angels in the giving of the law that prompted the writer of Hebrews to say so much about the superiority of Christ over angels. The revelation associated with the old covenant may have come to Moses through glorious angels, but the revelation associated with the new covenant has come to us through the eternal Son. The readers of the letter, who were tempted to draw back from full allegiance to Christ, needed to be reminded of the consequences of turning away from the truth of the gospel.

We must pay more careful attention, therefore, to what we have heard, so that we do not drift away. For if the message spoken by angels was binding, and every violation and disobedience received its just punishment, how shall we escape if we ignore such a great salvation? (Hebrews 2:1-2)

Participating in Worship

Another work of the angels in God's service is their care over the church. Angels seem to have particular interest in the operation and worship of the local church, the body of believers in a specific location.

When the apostle Paul wrote his disciple Timothy, the young man was pastor of the church at Ephesus. Paul devoted several sections of his first letter to instructions to Timothy about how to act as a shepherd of God's flock. The apostle concluded with this solemn charge: "I charge you, in the sight of God and Christ Jesus and the elect angels, to keep these instructions without partiality, and to do nothing out of favoritism" (1 Timothy 5:21). Paul was telling this young leader that God the Father and Jesus the Son were observing and evaluating his ministry to see if Timothy would be faithful in carrying out the principles Paul had set down. But in addition, Paul says God's holy angels were watching Timothy's service to God's people.

If angels watched over Timothy, they likewise watch over church leaders today, looking for faithfulness in our work and obedience to God's Word. What do angels find when they observe those of us who are elders or teachers or board members in the church? How much devotion to Christ do they see? How much obedience is evident in our lives? Their interest reminds us not to take lightly our positions in the church and our responsibility to those we minister to.

But angels observe more in the church than its leaders; they are curious also about our worship services. In 1 Corinthians 11 Paul writes one of the most controversial passages in the New Testament. He says that women should come to worship services with their heads covered. I don't want to get involved in *that* controversy! I simply want you to see one of the reasons Paul gives for being concerned that things are done properly in our church services. "For this reason, *and because of the angels*, the woman ought to have a sign of authority on her head" (11:10). Here and elsewhere in his Word God speaks about how men and women are to relate to each other in public worship. Angels watch to see how well we obey God's directions.

We can conclude, then, that our obedience in worship affects the angels as they worship God in fellowship with us. The Book of Common Prayer acknowledges the fact that angels are fellow worshipers with these marvelous words of the pastor in the celebration of Holy Communion: "Therefore, with Angels and Archangels, and with all the company of heaven, we laud and magnify thy glorious Name."[2]

The holy angels of God are vitally concerned with the oversight and worship of God's people. That fact should prompt all of us to view our participation and faithfulness more seriously than ever. No matter how small the congregation on Sunday, angels are present when God's people gather.

Making Room in the Bulletin

Wonderful guests are present every week in our worship services, yet we almost never recognize them. How can we in a practical and reverent way acknowledge the presence of angels? Let me suggest several approaches.

We have to begin by laying a foundation of biblical knowledge. Pastors or teachers could devote a series of messages or a Bible study to the work of God's holy angels. When the pastor or worship leader directs the congregation in public prayer, he or she could refer to the presence of angels and the worship which the angels lift to God. Several of our hymns acknowledge the work of angels (although, unfortunately, it is usually in sappy, emotional terms). Worship leaders may want to choose hymns or worship choruses that include angels and point out the fact that angels are present with God's people to worship the Lord. Another way to include angels in our arena of worship is to choose a Scripture reading or a call to worship that refers to God's holy angels and their presence with us in the church or before God's throne. Obviously the attention we draw to holy angels should never crowd out our adoration or worship of God alone. But what a joyous privilege it is to *share* in God's worship each week with such magnificent beings!

Since their creation, holy angels have surrounded the throne of God. They wait expectantly for his commands. They worship constantly before him. One of the great ancient declarations of faith is called Te Deum (from its original Latin form).[3] It expresses beautifully the attitude that should fill our hearts as we, with all of God's angels, come deliberately and confidently before our God in worship:

> We praise Thee, O God;
> We acknowledge Thee to be the Lord.
> All the earth doth worship Thee, the Father everlasting.
> To Thee all angels cry aloud;
> The heavens and all the powers therein.
> To Thee cherubim and seraphim continually do cry:
> Holy, Holy, Holy, Lord God of Sabaoth.
> Heaven and earth are full of the majesty of Thy glory.

CHAPTER TWELVE

They Will Lift You Up in Their Hands

GUARDIAN ANGELS

I LOVE TO TALK ABOUT ANGELS. Whenever I get to speak on the subject, I can count on one question from those who attend. The most asked question is "Do you believe that we have guardian angels?"

God's angels are such wonderful beings that we all want one we can claim as our own. That certainly explains much of the popular appeal of the New Age angel movement in our culture. Books and seminars taught by angel guides promise to introduce you to your own personal angel. One leader even assures you that you will learn your angel's name. I'm sorry if this disappoints you, but claims like that are not based on biblical truth.

The Bible does make it clear, however, that angels are charged with the ministry of guarding and preserving God's people. Beverly Bunch can vouch for that. When her children were small, she picked them up one day after school to take them to the dentist. The temperature outside was about forty degrees, and it was raining. As she left Route 60 to get on Interstate 64 in Huntington, West Virginia, she discovered that the bridge back over Route 60 was a sheet of ice. Her car slid toward the median of the bridge and could easily have plunged down onto the road below.

Beverly couldn't move the car because she couldn't control it. She was afraid that if she tried to move she would get herself and her children in a worse situation. She also realized that she couldn't simply stay where she was because other cars would slide as she had done and collide with her car. She got out of the car and tried to warn other drivers by waving her arms. A police car stopped, but he had to move on because of several accidents on the highway ahead. Beverly was desperate.

Just then a truck passed over the bridge in the opposite direction. When the driver saw Beverly's predicament, he pulled his truck over, walked across the icy bridge and offered to help. Even though it went against everything Beverly had been told about letting a stranger drive her car, she let the man drive over the bridge and back off the interstate on the other side. The car seemed to be fully controlled.

When the car was safely back on Route 60, the man got out and walked back to his truck. Beverly's testimony is clear: "He seemed to appear out of nowhere. I didn't know how to thank him or get in touch with him. I have always believed he was a guardian angel."

Obviously the man could have been human, someone prompted by compassion to stop and help. People with a skeptical bent will remove anything supernatural from the story, but Beverly Bunch won't be convinced otherwise. In the man's calming presence and expert control of the car in a very precarious situation, she sensed the presence of a protecting angel.

Some Biblical Clues

If you look for a Scripture verse that says, "Every Christian (or every person) has a guardian angel," you won't find one. But the Bible does give us some significant clues that lead us to conclude that angels are actively watching over us. For example, God gave a general promise to his people in the Old Testament about how angels would care for them:

If you make the Most High your dwelling—
    even the LORD, who is my refuge—
then no harm will befall you,
    no disaster will come near your tent.

For he will command his angels concerning you
    to guard you in all your ways;
they will lift you up in their hands,
    so that you will not strike your foot against a stone.

(Psalm 91:9-12)

A powerful Old Testament example of God's protecting angels is when the king's administrators threw Daniel the prophet into the lions' den. Miraculously, he lived through the night. At first light Daniel testified to the king of God's wondrous protection and his mastery over the wild beasts: "My God sent his angel, and he shut the mouths of the lions" (Daniel 6:22).

In the New Testament record angels function in the same way toward Christian believers. Shortly after Pentecost, the Jewish council imprisoned the apostles and planned to put them on trial the next day. "But during the night an angel of the Lord opened the doors of the jail and brought them out" (Acts 5:19). Several years later when Peter was imprisoned, an angel of the Lord appeared in Peter's cell and led him to safety outside the prison (Acts 12:5-11). In the middle of a torrential storm at sea, an angel of God stood beside the apostle Paul and assured him that all on board the ship would survive, even though the ship would be destroyed. When the ship went down, everyone reached land safely (Acts 27:23-44). Undoubtedly, each man was buoyed along by a protecting angel.

As wonderful as these biblical examples are, what we want to know is, Do angels guard and protect *us* in the same way? I have found only hints in Scripture, but the hints indicate that we do have guardian angels.

In Matthew 18, for example, Jesus talked to his disciples about the importance of children in God's program. Jesus included in his teaching an interesting statement about angels and children: "See that you do not look down on one of these little ones. For I tell you that their angels in heaven always see the face of my Father in heaven" (18:10). Apparently, some of God's angels are assigned to stand prepared before the Father to respond instantly to his command for protection and care over these children. Jesus calls these particular angels *"their* [the children's] angels."

Craig Keener in his commentary on the cultural background of the New Testament adds this insight:

> [It was believed that] angels received their orders from God's throne; but unlike lower angels and mortals, only the highest angels regularly saw God's glory. Those who mistreated these "little ones" would hence be reported directly to God by the greatest angels, and the report would stand them in bad stead in the day of judgment.[1]

Another hint about guardian angels comes from the incident in Acts 12, in which Peter was released from prison by an angel. Once outside the prison, Peter hurried to the home where a group of believers were praying earnestly for his release. When Peter knocked at the outer gate, a servant girl named Rhoda came to answer the door. At hearing Peter's voice, however, she was so overcome with joy that she ran back into the house without opening the outer door. She interrupted the prayer meeting with a shout: "Peter is at the door!"

The assembled believers at first disbelieved her: "You're out of your mind." When she kept insisting, their next words were "It must be *his angel*" (Acts 12:14-15). Their statement reflects the belief that every person has a personal angel who ministers to them and that, if the angel reveals himself, he looks and sounds much like the person under his care. The Christians gathered for this prayer meeting were sure that Peter had been killed in prison and that "his angel" had come to tell them about his death. What a surprise to open the door and find the real Peter—not dead but alive, thanks to an angel.

Protection and the Will of God

I conclude from the passages above that every believer has an angel assigned to him or her for life. That angel is responsible to guard and preserve that believer *when it is the will of God to do so.* I think we will stand before the Lord someday, and he will open our eyes on events in our lives so we will see his care and wisdom in every step we took. You and I will be astonished at how many times holy angels ministered to us and intervened for us.

Emily Pytyck, a dorm mother at Briercrest College in Saskatchewan, Canada, works in the summers as a cook at Dorion Bible Camp near Thunder Bay, Ontario. One summer in the early 1980s Emily used her day off to go into the nearby town of Dorion to do some shopping. Her last stop was at a gem shop on the main highway back to camp. As Emily left the shop's parking lot, she stopped and looked both directions on the highway. It looked clear for her left-hand turn. But just as she pushed on the accelerator to go on her way, she heard two powerful knocks on the trunk of her car. She slammed on her brakes and turned around to see who was behind her. No one was there. As she wheeled around toward the front of the car, a semi truck roared past her. If Emily had pulled out, she probably would have been killed. She bowed her head right there and thanked God for his protection. That evening when Emily got back to the camp, she was reading Psalm 34 in her devotions and she came upon verse 7: "The angel of the LORD encamps around those who fear him, and he delivers them." It was then that Emily realized that God had protected her that day through the intervention of one of his mighty angels.

The protection of angels doesn't mean, of course, that we will never be injured or killed. God sets the boundaries of our lives, and God's will for you or me may include injury or disability. We can take comfort in the fact, however, that nothing touches us except by God's permission. We owe a tremendous debt to the angels for their loving, diligent care.

Protecting God's Work

Perhaps (and I'm indulging again in some sanctified speculation) God assigns angelic protection over certain institutions too. We've already seen the intense interest and involvement of angels in the local church. If there are "angels of the churches" (Revelation 1:20), is it too far-fetched to believe that God assigns angels to watch over particular ministries that help the church to carry out his work in the world? Mission agencies, campus ministries, seminaries and Christian colleges all have stories to tell of God's unique care and provision. Sometimes those gifts have come through the intervention of angels.

One such ministry is a Christian camp in Michigan's northern woods, located about one hundred miles north of where I live. Camp Barakel has touched the lives of thousands and thousands of children, young people and adults. The camp was founded over forty years ago by Holman "Johnnie" Johnson. I've had the privilege of speaking there several times, and I'm always impressed by the quiet serenity of the place.

God has worked many miracles to provide for and sustain the ministry of Camp Barakel, but one in particular stands out. It happened in the summer of 1976 when a forest fire started in the Huron National Forest northwest of the camp's property. As the fire moved closer, Johnnie Johnson and a few camp staffers went to the northwest corner of the property to see if they could do anything to protect the camp. The smoke was so thick they had to lie down occasionally to breathe the fresh air near the ground's surface. All they could do was pray.

When they got up from prayer, a man in a yellow fire suit driving a yellow bulldozer roared out of the smoke. He was pulling a seven-foot-wide fire plow. "Where should I go?" he asked. "Which direction?" Johnnie pointed the man in the direction of their north property line. The driver made two cuts along that line, turning up a fourteen-foot firebreak. Then Johnnie turned the man down the west property line. With this help, the fire stopped at Barakel's property.

During the next few days Johnnie tried repeatedly to find out who the man on the bulldozer was and where he came from. None of the crews or agencies that fought the fire knew anything about the man. No one from the camp saw him leave or load his equipment on a truck. The firebreak line just ended near the road.[2]

It's possible, of course, that the man was just a firefighter whom God providentially moved to the right spot at the right time. That would have been a miracle in itself. But it is equally possible that an angel of God in response to earnest prayer provided for these faithful servants of God what was beyond their own means.

Should I Look for an Angel?

The second most frequently asked question whenever I talk with people about angels is "Have *you* ever seen an angel?" My answer (a least up to now) is that I have never personally seen an angel. I believe I *have* however, been the object of angelic care and protection. When I was in college, I came home one evening from a late class in the middle of a blustery Michigan blizzard. As I crossed a slippery overpass, the two cars that were side by side in front of me collided. I tried to stop, but instead my car began to skid on the icy pavement. As I headed for a serious crash, the two cars in front of me skidded apart. My own steering wheel was jerked to the left, and my vehicle went between the two cars without a scratch. I can still remember (twenty-five years later) sitting beside the road and staring at the steering wheel. I knew that someone other than me had been controlling the car. I gave thanks to God for his protection. I firmly believe that he stationed an angel to secure my protection and perhaps my survival.

That story leads me to another issue that seems to perplex many Christians: Why do some people receive the direct ministry of angels and others do not? Why do some Christians even have the privilege of seeing an angel while most of us will never see one (in this life anyway)?

The answer to those questions, of course, is hidden in the will of God. We may as well ask, Why are some faithful devoted Christians healed of cancer while other Christians who are just as faithful and just as devoted to the Lord die from cancer? Is God playing favorites? Of course not.

I have a dear friend who was pronounced dead in the emergency room of the hospital. At the insistence of a nurse who knew my friend, the medical staff worked to revive her. Her heart was restarted, and after several hours they were able to stabilize her condition. When her husband, Don, came into the room, she was talking about a beautiful city. Don's words in response were "She's been there." Ione Turcott is persuaded that she was taken to heaven and given a glimpse of its glory. Then, for some reason unknown to her, she was sent back to this life.

Ione is not a kook, and she is not a person given to extremes. She is a faithful, humble servant of God who in quiet ways has helped more people and supported God's work more generously than any Christian I have ever known. God had given Ione a preview of her eternal home.

I have never seen heaven. Does God love Ione more than he loves me? Should I pray that God will give me the same experience she had? Should I feel second-rate in God's program if he doesn't give me the same vision of heaven? Even asking the questions is absurd.

Nowhere in the Bible does God tell us to seek or to pray that he will let us see his angels. On rare occasions God gives a believer a glimpse of an angelic visitor. We should rejoice with those who have genuine encounters with angels. But if God never gives you or me the same experience, we should not be discouraged. We can be assured from God's Word that his angels do guard us and, at times, lift us up in their hands.

CHAPTER THIRTEEN

Some Have Entertained Angels Unawares

ANGELS AND US

UTSUKO HASEGAWA CAME TO BELIEVE in the Lord Jesus Christ through the ministry of a young American missionary, Mabel Francis. Mutsuko's father was the mayor of Hiroshima, Japan. Her desire was to be a missionary like Miss Francis. That desire was dashed, however, when she learned that her parents had already arranged her marriage to a non-Christian man.

In time Mutsuko received assurance in her heart that the Lord would work even in this event for her good and for his glory. Three daughters were born to Mutsuko and her husband. Then World War II began. Her husband went into the army to fight for the emperor and eventually lost his life in the war.

The day Mutsuko learned of her husband's death, her first thought was to commit suicide. But suddenly Mutsuko heard the Lord's voice in her mind. "You wanted to be a missionary, didn't you? Can't you raise these girls to be missionaries for me?"

She returned to Hiroshima and began to work for her sister-in-law, a doctor in the city. Her life seemed back on track. But soon she began to sense another command. It was so persistent that it seemed almost audible: "Escape to the mountain, escape to the mountain."

Hiroshima had not been a military target at any time during the war, and yet

Mutsuko knew that Japan was preparing for a final stand as the Allied forces drew nearer. The insistent words kept coming: "Escape to the mountain, escape to the mountain!" Finally Mutsuko obeyed. She gathered up her children and a few belongings and, in a hired truck, left Hiroshima.

At 8:16 the next morning, a blinding flash and a mushroom cloud engulfed Hiroshima. Like Lot and his family in the Old Testament, Mutsuko watched the destruction from the far-off mountains. She believed that God's angels had led her and her three potential missionaries to safety.[1]

The primary work of angels for us believers is guarding and protecting us. But we find glimpses of several other ministries as we read the pages of Scripture. One of those ministries is the ministry of guidance—a work that Mutsuko Hasegawa will never forget.

Angels and Guidance

Several times in Scripture God used angels to direct his people. As the Israelites left Egypt to go to the land of Canaan, God promised supernatural guidance for their journey. "See, I am sending an angel ahead of you to guard you along the way and to bring you to the place I have prepared" (Exodus 23:20; see also Exodus 32:34; 33:2; Isaiah 63:9).

Individual believers also benefit from angelic direction. Three times an angel appeared to Joseph to give him specific instructions about the protection and care of Jesus. Twice in the book of Acts angels guided the expanding outreach of the gospel to the Gentiles. First, an angel directed Philip to go to the road between Jerusalem and Gaza. On that road the Holy Spirit led Philip to an Ethiopian eunuch, who, in response to Philip's witness, believed in Christ and then took the message of the gospel to his own people (Acts 8:26-29). On the other occasion, an angel told Cornelius, a Gentile who was seeking after God, to send for Peter, who would tell him how to be saved (Acts 10:3-6; 11:13-14).

But specific instruction came to Peter by the Holy Spirit (10:19-20; 11:12).

It is significant in each case that an angel relayed instructions, but the Holy Spirit is the one who spoke with true authority. When the Spirit told Peter that three men were waiting to take him to Cornelius, he added, "Do not hesitate to go with them, for *I* have sent them" (Acts 10:20). Believers are guided primarily by the Spirit of God (Acts 16:6-7; Galatians 5:18). It would be a serious mistake to wait for guidance from an angel when you are faced with a serious decision. God certainly *can* use angels to give us direction if he chooses, but his preferred method of guidance is the voice of the Spirit within us.

Angels are not a substitute for the Holy Spirit. (What a poor substitute they would be!) The ministry of angels is primarily external, while the Spirit's ministry is internal. Angels focus on the physical realm as they guard our bodies and pathways. The Spirit focuses on the spiritual realm as he guards our spirits and leads us in the right way. The angels may be agents to answer prayer, but the Spirit prompts and directs prayer within us (Romans 8:26-27; Jude 20).[2]

Angels and Prayer

There's another ministry of angels that I do not fully understand, but God's Word reveals its truth. In addition to being used by God to answer the prayers of believers, holy angels also assist those prayers in some way as they are offered to God. Please do not conclude from this statement that we are to pray to angels. The New Testament pattern is to pray to God the Father through the Lord Jesus in the power of the Spirit. But somehow as we offer prayer up to God, the angels assist in that process.

The clearest example of this ministry is found in Revelation 8:

Another angel, who had a golden censer, came and stood at the altar. He was given much incense to offer, with the prayers of all the saints, on the golden altar before the throne. The smoke of the incense, together with the prayers of the saints, went up before God from the angel's hand. (vv. 3-4; compare also Revelation 5:8)

While the angel is involved in presenting the prayers of the saints to God, the angel does not make them acceptable to God in any way. Some Jewish writers of the New Testament era taught that angels acted as mediators between God and human beings, but the New Testament writers totally reject that idea.[3] Angels do not plead our cause before the Father or intercede for us, but they do play a part in offering our prayers up to God.

Angels and Death

As Jesus told the story of a wealthy man and Lazarus, a poor beggar, he gave us a wonderful insight into the ministry of angels to us at the time of death. Angels carry the spirits of believers who have died to a place of rest and blessing. In Jesus' story Lazarus was a believer. He was poor materially but had been declared righteous before God. When he died, "the angels carried him to Abraham's side" (Luke 16:22). I believe that is still a ministry of angels to those who are saved by God's grace. Today the spirits of believers who die go immediately into the presence of Christ (Philippians 1:23; 2 Corinthians 5:8), but we don't leave this life alone. God sends powerful invisible agents who transport us to the realm of heaven, to the Father's house.

Angels Around Us

The final ministry of angels toward us is the one that captivates our interest the most. Angels can, at times, appear in human form to help or to comfort believers. The writer of Hebrews, who knew so much about angels, added this admonition about them at the end of his letter:

Keep on loving each other as brothers. Do not forget to entertain strangers, for by so doing some people have entertained angels without knowing it. (Hebrews 13:1-2)

Some interpreters of Scripture believe that the writer of Hebrews is simply referring back to Abraham's visit from angels in Genesis 18 and Lot's encounter with the angels in Genesis 19 as illustrations of how we should show hospitality to each other. I think that interpretation restricts the passage too much. It seems clear to me that the writer accepted the possibility that we may at times encounter angels who appear as human beings but who are present to help us or to bless us in some way. Our response to that stranger we meet may determine whether the blessing or help is received or lost. Don't ignore the possibility that God may send an angel into your path.

Dave Thompson pastors a growing church in Pocatello, Idaho. In 1977, when Dave lived in Kalamazoo, Michigan, one of our winter storms blasted through the area. He drove his wife to a nearby grocery store to renew their milk and munchies supply at home. The store parking lot was almost deserted, and they parked close to the door. As soon as his wife entered the store, Dave was startled by a knock on the window of his car. He rolled the window down a crack and an elderly woman asked him if he knew of a place where she could get a flat tire fixed. He said, "Well, there's an Amoco station down the street. I'm sure there is a phone in the store here. You could call them." The woman went into the grocery store, and instantly Dave felt convicted by the Lord. He should have offered to help. He got out of the car, intending to find the woman and offer his assistance. When he entered the store, however, no one was at the pay phone inside the door. Dave searched the aisles of the nearly empty store looking for the woman. He even sent his wife, Mary, into the ladies' restroom, but the woman wasn't found. No one he asked had even seen the woman he described. Dave and Mary drove all around the area of the store, looking for a vehicle with a flat tire, but they found none. Dave is convinced that the woman was an angel who had come to minister to him in some way, but the opportunity was now lost. "I had to confess to God," he says, "that I had been in the presence of an angel and had blown it!"

I'm not advocating that you pick up every hitchhiker in the hope that you will find an angel sitting beside you. We are always to exercise wisdom. But when God opens a door for you to entertain or care for a stranger, embrace that opportunity as a wonderful privilege. You will reap the blessing of obedience to God, and you may discover yourself blessed richly in return.

I grew up in a pastor's home. We never had much money, but my parents were always bringing new people home from church for Sunday dinner or using my bedroom to house a missionary family who was traveling through the area. My parents still consider it a special privilege to have missionaries or conference speakers into their home. They never ask for recognition or reimbursement. They just do it for the joy of serving. I'm certain that over the years some angels have found lodging and fellowship in their gracious home.

I hope that this study of angels has helped you to understand these marvelous beings better. I hope, too, that you will appreciate more than ever before all that God has done for your blessing and benefit through his angels. Most of all, I hope you will be more open each day to the possibility of angelic ministry in your life. Angels *are* all around us!

~ Name and Subject Index ~

∽ Scripture Index ∽

Scripture Index

1:6-7 59
2:1 4, 64
2:1-2 59
38 26
38:4-7 25

Psalms
5:4-5 59
8:3 58
18:10 45
34:7 81, 100
68:17 4
80:1 44
89:6-8 4
89:7 4
91:9-12 98
91:11-12 74
99:1 44
101:3 37
103:20-21 4, 91
148:1-5 21-22
148:2 4

Isaiah
6 42
6:2 15
6:3 90
6:7 42
14:3 53
14:9-11 53
14:12-15 26, 53
14:13 54
14:14 28
63:9 106

Ezekiel
1:5-6 15
1:4-14 44
1:22-26 44
1:28 44
10:20 44
10:21 15
28:9 45
28:12-17 45-46
28:14-16 58
40:3-4 91
41:17-20 44

Daniel
3:25 48
3:28 48
4:13 4
4:17 4
4:23 4
6:22 31, 98
7:10 40
8:13 4
8:15 48
8:16-17 34
8:17-19 91
9:21 34
9:21-22 48, 91
10 119
10:11-13 34
10:13 47
10:20 35
10:21 47
12:1 47

Habakkuk
1:13 59

Zechariah
1:9 118
1:11-12 81
1:14-17 91
2:3 118
3:1-2 81
3:3 118
4:1-6 81
5:9 118
6:5-6 118
14:5 4

Matthew
1:20 81
1:20-23 73
2:13-20 73
4:1 73
4:1-11 37
4:6 74
4:8-10 35
4:11 74
5:17-18 3
5:29-30 85
6:26 58
6:34 37
8:28-29 33
8:29 67
12:22 76
12:24 55, 75
12:26 75
12:28 75
12:32 75
12:45 76
13:36-41 5
13:37-42 79

Romans

1:26-27 65
5:12 55
5:17 55
8:26-27 107
8:31 60
8:33 60
8:37 60
8:38 36

1 Corinthians

2:10 37
6:2-3 84
10:20 85
11:10 94
15:49 83

2 Corinthians

2:11 57
5:8 108
11:14 52
12:2 58

Galatians

3:19 92
5:18 107

Ephesians

1:7-8 88
2:2 58
2:8-9 88
2:13 88
3:10 49
6:10-11 36
6:12 14, 48

6:13 36
6:17 36
6:18 37

Philippians

1:23 108
2:10-11 68
4:8 85
4:19 37

Colossians

1:13 55
1:15-17 22, 70
1:16 48
2:10 49
2:15 89
2:18 84

1 Thessalonians

4:16 46, 78

2 Thessalonians

1:7 78

1 Timothy

2:1-2 35
3:6 27
4:1 57
5:21 55, 93

Hebrews

1:3-4 72
1:6 71
1:14 14, 88
2:1-2 93

2:5-8 83
2:5-9 71
2:14-16 88
5:7 38
9:12 60
10:10 60
10:12 60
10:14 60
13:1-2 109

James

2:25 4

1 Peter

1:10-12 89
5:8 63

2 Peter

1:19 12
2:4 62, 89
2:10-11 31

1 John

2:1-2 60
3:2 83
4:1-3, 12
4:4 32
5:19 35

Jude

6 63
7 65
8-10 32
9 46
20 107

~ *Afterword* ~

I AM INTERESTED IN HEARING about your own encounters with angels or about your own reflections on the ministries of angels. I am also available to present "Angels Around Us" seminars in churches or for Christian organizations. If you are interested in sponsoring a seminar or have other comments, please to write me at this address:

Douglas Connelly
"Angels Around Us" Seminar
c/o InterVarsity Press
P.O. Box 1400
Downers Grove, Illinois 60515

∼ *Notes* ∼

Chapter 3: Are They Not All Ministering Spirits?

1. Some Bible scholars believe that in Zechariah 5:9 the two women who carry away the wickedness of Israel are angels. They are agents of divine judgment, but, in a highly symbolic vision, it is difficult to say that they are angels. The women have the wings of a stork (an unclean bird according to Leviticus 11:19), and they carry a third woman (symbolizing wickedness) to Babylon. Angels do appear in Zechariah's other visions, but they are always identified clearly as angels (compare Zechariah 1:9; 2:3; 3:3; 6:5-6).

Chapter 4: All the Sons of God Shouted for Joy

1. See also Matthew 22:23-33 and Luke 20:27-40. Resurrected human beings will no longer need procreation to sustain the human race. The phrase "neither marry nor be given in marriage" does not refer simply to the relationship of marriage but to the procreative and reproductive aspects within marriage. See Robert Gundry, *Matthew: A Commentary on His Literary and Theological Art* (Grand Rapids, Mich.: Eerdmans, 1982), p. 446; and Ezra Gould, *A Critical and Exegetical Commentary on the Gospel According to Mark*, International Critical Commentaries (reprint, Edinburgh: T & T Clark, 1975), p. 229.

2. This idea of human beings becoming angels also has roots in Jewish and Christian mythology. According to the apocryphal Prayer of Joseph, Jacob was transformed into the angel Uriel, the "archangel of the power of the Lord." Christian legends have St. Francis evolving into the angel Rhamiel, and Anne, the Virgin Mary's mother, becoming the angel Anas.

3. These legends are drawn from Louis Ginzberg, *The Legends of the Jews* (Philadelphia: Jewish Publication Society of America, 1968).

4. Many modern commentators on Isaiah reject the idea that this passage contains a cryptic description of Satan's fall. See, for example, John Oswalt, *The Book of Isaiah: Chapters 1-39*, New International Commentary on the Old Testament (Grand Rapids, Mich.: Eerdmans,

1986), p. 320. These writers view Isaiah's words as merely the exaggerated claims of the Babylonian king. It seems clearer to me, however (in agreement with early church fathers as well as some contemporary scholars), to see Isaiah moving from a description of the pride and fall of the earthly king to a statement of the pride and fall of the angelic prince of this world. If we believe that the prophets were given divine insight into events future to their time, why can't we accept their insights into events long before their time? See Herbert Wolf, *Interpreting Isaiah* (Grand Rapids, Mich.: Zondervan, 1985), p. 113; and Alfred Martin and John Martin, *Isaiah: The Glory of the Messiah* (Chicago: Moody Press, 1983), pp. 72ff.

5. You will find a fascinating compilation of angel names and legends from several religions and traditions in Gustav Davidson, *A Dictionary of Angels* (New York: Macmillan/Free Press, 1967).

Chapter 5: And I Saw a Strong Angel

1. Many Bible teachers believe that Daniel saw a theophany, an appearance of the Lord Jesus in his preincarnate glory. See John Walvoord, *Daniel: The Key to Prophetic Revelation* (Chicago: Moody Press, 1971), pp. 242-45; Renald Showers, *The Most High God: A Commentary on the Book of Daniel* (Bellmawr, N.J.: The Friends of Israel Gospel Ministry, 1982), pp. 141ff.; and Ronald Wallace, *The Lord Is King: The Message of Daniel* (Downers Grove, Ill.: InterVarsity Press, 1979), pp. 173-74. It is difficult to accept, however, that God himself was hindered on his mission by an evil angel, "the prince of the Persian kingdom." Some commentators (Walvoord, Wallace) distinguish between the man Daniel saw in 10:5-6 (identified as God) and the man who spoke to Daniel in 10:11Œ12:13 (identified as an angel). The text certainly doesn't make that distinction. Other students (Showers) see Christ as the man all the way through the passage but insist that even Christ could be hindered by an evil angel if God providentially permitted it. I conclude like other students of Daniel (Joyce Baldwin, *Daniel*, Tyndale Old Testament Commentaries [Downers Grove, Ill.: InterVarsity Press, 1978], p. 180; and John Goldingay, *Daniel*, Word Biblical Commentary [Waco, Tex.: Word, 1989], p. 291) that Daniel saw a glorious angel who came and spoke to him.

Chapter 6: Angelic Majesties

1. Malcolm Godwin, *Angels: An Endangered Species* (New York: Simon & Schuster, 1990), pp. 23ff.

2. *The Book of Enoch*, trans. R. H. Charles (London: SPCK, 1970), passim.

3. *The War Rule* (1QM, 4QM), 15. 14; 17. 6-7. G. Vermes, *The Dead Sea Scrolls in English*, 3rd ed. (London: Penguin Books, 1990).

4. Several other references to Michael in art and literature can be found in Gustav Davidson, *A Dictionary of Angels* (New York: Macmillan/Free Press, 1967), pp. 193ff.
5. The complete story of John Paton's life can be found in John G. Paton, *Missionary to the New Hebrides* (reprint, London: Banner of Truth Trust, 1965).

Chapter 7: The Devil and His Angels
1. See note 4 from chapter 4.
2. I am indebted for some of these insights to Renald Showers, who is on the staff of the Friends of Israel Gospel Ministry. His teaching was presented in a series of taped lectures at the Moody Keswick Bible Conference in St. Petersburg, Florida.
3. For an entertaining (and sobering) account of the danger of confronting demons in our own power, read Acts 19:11-16.

Chapter 8: Bound with Everlasting Chains
1. See Richard Bauckham, *Jude, 2 Peter*, Word Biblical Commentary (Waco, Tex.: Word, 1983), p. 249.
2. Probably the most reasoned defense of this view is in John Murray, *Principles of Conduct* (Grand Rapids, Mich.: Eerdmans, 1957), pp. 243-49.
3. See Gordon J. Wenham, *Genesis 1-15*, Word Biblical Commentary (Waco, Tex.: Word, 1987), pp. 139-41. For the position that angels possessed human beings, see Allen P. Ross, *Creation and Blessing: A Guide to the Study and Exposition of Genesis* (Grand Rapids, Mich.: Baker, 1988), pp. 181-83. For a presentation of all the possibilities, see Victor Hamilton, *The Book of Genesis: Chapter 1-17*, New International Commentary on the Old Testament (Grand Rapids, Mich.: Eerdmans, 1990), pp. 261-72.
4. The book of Enoch is dated about 200 b.c. It is a long, apocryphal book, but it reflects the prevailing opinion among the Jews of that era. The same view (that angels were involved in Genesis 6) is reflected abundantly in other Jewish literature of that period (*1 Enoch* 6-19; 21; 86-88; 106:13-15, 17; *Jubilees* 4:15, 22; 5:1; *Targum of Pseudo-Jonathan*; *Testament of Reuben* 5:6-7; *Testament of Naphtali* 3:5; Genesis Apocryphon [1Q apGen] 2:1). See Richard Bauckham, *Jude, 2 Peter*, Word Biblical Commentary (Waco, Tex.: Word, 1983), pp. 51ff, for a detailed discussion of this literature and its bearing on this interpretive issue.
5. See Maxwell Coder, *Jude: The Acts of the Apostates* (Chicago: Moody Press, 1958), p. 38.

Chapter 9: An Angel Strengthened Him
1. An excellent discussion of the correlation between the angel of the Lord and Jesus Christ

can be found in Ron Rhodes, *Christ Before the Manger: The Life and Times of the Preincarnate Christ* (Grand Rapids, Mich.: Baker, 1992), pp. 79ff.

Chapter 11: In the Council of His Holy Ones

1. This insight was expressed by Renald Showers in a series of lectures on angels given at the Moody Keswick Conference in St. Petersburg, Florida.
2. The Book of Common Prayer (1928 ed.), p. 77.
3. The Te Deum can be found in many worship manuals and hymn books. This version came from *Hymns for the Family of God* (Nashville: Paragon, 1976), #324.

Chapter 12: They Will Lift You Up in Their Hands

1. Craig Keener, *The IVP Bible Background Commentary: New Testament* (Downers Grove, Ill.: InterVarsity Press, 1993), p. 93.
2. This story comes from a personal conversation in 1994 with Johnnie Johnson. It is also recorded in his earlier self-published book about the camp, *Barakel: God's Miracle* (P.O. Box 157, Fairview, Michigan 48621-0157).

Chapter 13: Some Have Entertained Angels Unawares

1. This story comes from L. W. Northrup, *Encounters with Angels* (Wheaton, Ill.: Tyndale, 1988), pp. 45-48.
2. This comparison between the Spirit and angels is drawn from C. Fred Dickason, *Angels: Elect and Evil* (Chicago: Moody Press, 1975), p. 101.
3. Compare Tobit 12:15; 3 Baruch 11; contrast 1 Timothy 2:5.

There's an
Angel
on Your
Shoulder

*Angel Encounters
in Everyday Life*

KELSEY TYLER

CARMEL • NEW YORK 10512

THERE'S AN ANGEL ON YOUR SHOULDER

This Guideposts edition is published by special arrangement with The Berkley Publishing Group.

ISBN: 0-425-14369-4

Designed by José R. Fonfrias
PRINTED IN THE UNITED STATES OF AMERICA

~ *Acknowledgments* ~

THIS BOOK WOULD NOT HAVE BEEN POSSIBLE without the numerous people who contributed their stories to my effort. I wish to thank each of them and assure them that a purpose has been served in making these stories public. Thanks to Maria Amato for uprooting herself and taking special care of my children during those intense writing times. You are the best, Moe!

I want to thank my husband for encouraging me to turn my dreams into realities, and my children for showing me a little bit of Heaven every day. Also, thanks go to my parents, who continue to be my primary source of feedback, and to my forever friends—Susan Kane, Pat Winning, Jo Ann, and Amber— who heard this book before I put it into print and who believed, as I did, that every one of these angel encounters was possible. I sure miss you all!

*This book is dedicated to
the family of Christian believers
around the world,
especially those of you who
have truly helped me in
my walk of faith.*

*And to our Savior and Lord,
Jesus Christ*

*May we all be encouraged
daily by His
guiding hands and
mysterious ways,
even perhaps by His
angels.*

~ A Note to the Reader ~

*Are not all angels ministering spirits sent to
serve those who will inherit salvation?*

HEBREWS 1:14

SEVERAL YEARS AGO I came across my first angel encounter. I was a new Christian at the time and was attending a camp at Angeles Crest, outside of Los Angeles, when I heard counselor Chris Smith tell an impressive story. For months afterward, I found myself sharing his story with other people, always amazed at the details.

After that I began to wonder. Was it possible that God really used angels to minister to those who believe in Him? In time, I began to hear more such stories. I started putting together a collection of angel encounters so that those who also had such experiences would know they were not alone; and so those of us who had not would be comforted by God's amazing presence around us, perhaps looking more closely the next time a stranger helps us on some deserted desert highway.

In putting this collection together, I had the privilege of talking to most of the people whose encounters are detailed in this book. In some instances, the people involved requested that they be referred to by pseudonyms to protect their privacy, and this has been done. On the few occasions when it was impossible to contact the people involved, the details were provided by someone who heard the story first-hand and believed it to be both truthful and completely credible. In these cases, names are fictitious and are not intended to represent specific living persons. However, it is not the intention of this book to prove the validity of these angel encounters. Instead, they have been written for your pleasure, to evaluate and take at face value.

It is my prayer that you, the reader, will gain from these stories a deeper assurance of your personal faith and a comfort in knowing that God is near. Sometimes closer than you might ever imagine.

~ *Preface* ~

WHY IS MANKIND FASCINATED BY ANGELS? Songs sing about their presence, films bring to life their existence, and through the ages people have speculated about their possibility. When we put faith in scripture, as millions of people have done throughout the ages, we must at some point address the question of angels. If these heavenly messengers of God appeared to common people in biblical times, why would they not also appear today to those who believe they exist?

Science, for all its technological wisdom, has never proven the existence of angels. Perhaps the closest we will come to knowing the truth about angels is in sharing the fascinating and unexplainable angel encounters of others. For a time, angel encounters were described as sightings of winged beings, oftentimes robed in white or ethereal coverings. But in modern times, stories of such sightings have become more specific; the angels, more humanlike, their tasks, more immediate. These encounters tend to have in common mysterious people who perform a rescue or relay a message and then suddenly disappear without explanation. Often, people who have had such experiences will seek out the person who helped them, only to find that he or she never existed.

For instance, the time a woman sat crying and praying at the hospital bedside of her terminally ill husband and was comforted only when a male nurse entered the room and offered to sit with her. For more than an hour he comforted the woman, assuring her that her husband was going to be all right in the place he was going. The next morning, after her husband died, the woman asked about the male nurse, wanting to thank him for the comfort he had brought in those final hours. "Ma'am," she was told at the hospital desk, "we have no male nurses on staff."

The following pages contain a collection of these lifelike angel encounters, relayed in detail as accurately as possible. A few of the stories have become modern-day folklore, told time and again around the world. For these stories, much of the detail is not verifiable and can be taken only at face value as handed down from one person to the next.

Others, though, are entirely documented, complete with times, dates, names, and eyewitnesses. There is a remarkable similarity between these stories and those that cannot be documented. We are left to wonder whether the stranger who disappeared without an explanation might have, in fact, been an angel.

Miracle on the Mountain

❧

CHRIS SMITH HAD DRIVEN THE ROAD A HUNDRED TIMES. He had spent the past seven years as full-time counselor for Angeles Crest Christian Camp, a retreatlike cluster of cabins nestled 7,300 feet above sea level, atop the San Gabriel Mountains outside of Los Angeles. The winding, dangerous road was part of the life he and his family had chosen.

Since taking the job and moving to their mountaintop home, Chris, twenty-eight, and his wife, Michele, had watched their family grow. Their oldest child, Keagan, was now nearly five, Kailey was three, and Michele was five months pregnant with their third child. Chris and Michele loved the thought of raising a large family in their mountain cabin and couldn't have been happier.

Chris, blond with blue eyes and the good looks of a suntanned surfer, had no regrets about choosing such a secluded lifestyle for his family. With crime and overcrowding pressures in the city, their little mountain cabin suited him perfectly. He enjoyed the thrill of watching busloads of hassled people arrive at the camp each week and leave days later renewed in their faith and attitude. When work was over and Chris headed back toward the cabin, he and Michele would take the children for hikes to explore the wilderness around their home. Theirs was a rewarding life and one that he and his family had come to cherish.

On the warm summer afternoon of August 10, 1991, Chris finished organizing the details for the next group of campers and walked through tall pine trees to his cabin, adjacent to the main hall.

1

Michele's face lit up as he opened the door and entered the room. He smiled at her, amazed that she seemed to grow more beautiful each day.

"Finished?" she asked as he pulled her into a hug.

"For now. The campers will be here this evening."

It was 2:30 p.m. and there were still several hours before darkness would blanket the mountain. For a moment, Chris and Michele remained in an embrace, enjoying the solitude and closeness of each other. But suddenly a door opened near the back of the house and their two children came running into the main room.

"Daddy! Daddy!" Both children squealed with delight and raced toward Chris, jumping into his arms. "Play with us, come on, Daddy! Let's play tackle!"

Chris laughed. Keagan and Kailey were the joy of his life. The two blond children were full of energy and laughter and enjoyed nothing more than spending time rolling on the floor with their father. Chris could hardly wait until the new baby could join them in this ritual of afternoon play.

For thirty minutes Chris played with the children, laughing and tickling them until, finally, they lay stretched across the floor exhausted. Michele entered from the back of the cabin where she had been busy working in the kitchen, into the main room, humming to herself.

"What time are you going to town?" she asked. Chris jumped up nimbly and brushed a lock of hair from his forehead. "Five minutes," he said, grinning. Michele smiled to herself. She never got over how handsome he was, how he could bring a room to life with his smile. "I think I'll take Kailey with me this time."

Michele nodded. "OK," she said, smiling at their little girl.

Every week Chris drove down the winding mountainside for groceries and supplies. Usually he took Keagan with him so the two could spend some special time together. But now that Kailey was getting older, Chris thought it was time she was given a turn.

Michele crouched down so she could look into her daughter's eyes. "Kailey, you be a good girl for Daddy, hear?" The child nodded and Michele glanced up at Chris. "And you be careful, OK?"

"Always."

The two-lane highway was barely etched into the side of the mountain and was bordered by sheer clifflike drops of several hundred feet. It wound like a roller coaster up and down the mountain and left little room for error. Each year there were numerous fatalities along the twenty-five-mile stretch of roadway from the valley floor to the camp. The Smiths had known people who had been killed when their cars flipped over the side of the road and tumbled into the canyon below. Even someone like Chris, who knew every curve and straightaway of the road as if it belonged to him, could easily spend an hour of complete concentration while driving to the nearest market at the base of the mountain.

Chris smiled and swung his muscular arm around Michele's slim shoulder. "I've got to get some lumber for the camp, and I'll stop at the market," he said, mentally going over the items they needed. "Is there anything else you need?"

Michele shook her head. "I don't know. I've been with the kids all day. You're all I need right now."

Chris smiled again, bending to kiss his wife gently. "Don't worry, I'll be home before you know it. Come on, Kailey, let's get going," he said, motioning toward the little girl.

Kailey, every bit as beautiful as her mother but with a charm all her own, nodded seriously and then broke into a contagious smile as she skipped to her father's side. "Love you, Mommy," she said in her small voice, leaning up to kiss her mother. She would be four in a few months and was growing up quickly.

Michele hugged her daughter. "Love you, too, honey." Then she turned to Chris. "Drive safely," she said again. It was something she always said, something that could never be said enough.

"Always," he said, winking at her and pointing toward the heavens. Years earlier they had begun using the gesture as a way of reminding each other of their belief that prayer would keep them safely in God's hands. Michele returned the sign and smiled.

"See you soon," Chris said. He reached down for Kailey's hand and the two of them headed toward their brand-new Ford Ranger parked outside.

The day was beautiful: soothing rays of sunshine filtered through the pine trees, and the sky blazed a crystal-clear blue above. Chris hummed to himself as he buckled Kailey into her car seat, checking to be sure the car seat was attached securely to the backseat of the vehicle. He kissed her nose and tousled her hair before climbing into the driver's seat.

Nearly three hours later they had gotten all their supplies and were heading back up the mountainside when Chris began to feel the lumber shifting in the back of his vehicle. He slowed down enough to prevent the load from spilling over. The wood was tied down, but if the load spilled, the ropes would be useless and the lumber could tumble onto the highway. At about the same time, he reached a busy section of the narrow highway which served as a shortcut for commuters. Chris knew that a spill could trigger a dangerous accident; and he silently prayed that the load he was carrying would stay in place.

Many people lived in the desert community of Palmdale but worked in the Los Angeles basin. Typically, that commute took more than an hour in heavy traffic, but as much as twenty minutes could be saved by taking a mountain road that merges with Angeles Crest Highway for several miles. Chris knew, as did everyone who drove the mountain highway on a regular basis, how busy that section of the road could be.

Glancing in his rearview mirror, Chris saw that several impatient drivers had come up behind him. He tried to accelerate, but as he did, the lumber he was carrying shifted dangerously, and he was forced to slow down once more.

Kailey was singing to herself, unaware of the predicament her father was in. She sang in her sweet, high-pitched voice as Chris looked for a place to pull over. If only he could let the cars behind him pass, he could resume his drive at a slow pace and avoid spilling his load of lumber. He scanned the side of the highway in frustration. There were only inches separating the road from the canyon's edge, and there was no turnout for several miles.

He glanced once more in his mirror and worried that one of the drivers might try to pass him—a common cause of serious accidents along the highway. His eyes were off the road for just a moment. When he looked again, his truck was heading off the roadway. Terrified he might fall over the canyon edge, Chris made a split-second decision against slamming on his brakes. The other cars were following too closely, and if they hit him, the impact could send him over the cliff. Instead, he pulled over toward the shoulder—less than three feet wide at that location—and applied the brakes slowly. The other cars began to pass him and Chris sighed aloud. He tried not to think what might have happened if he hadn't looked ahead when he did.

Then, just before his vehicle came to a complete stop, the earth under his front right tire gave way and, in an instant, the Ranger began tumbling down the mountainside into the canyon.

"Hold on!" he screamed. Somewhere in the distance he could hear Kailey crying.

The Ranger tumbled wildly downward, and Chris was struck by an uncontrollable force which slammed his body against the shoulder harness of his seat belt and then against his truck's shell with each complete roll. As his vehicle continued bouncing and rolling down the mountain, Chris could feel his head swelling. He knew he would probably not live through the accident, but his biggest fear was for Kailey, whose cries had eerily disappeared.

Finally, more than 500 feet down the mountain, Chris's Ranger came to rest upside down. Chris was trapped in the front seat, but he was conscious. A warm liquid was oozing around his eyes and mouth and ears; he knew, without looking, that he was bleeding badly.

"Kailey!" he screamed, desperately trying to maneuver his body so he could see the child. "Kailey, baby, where are you?"

Chris listened intently but heard only the sound of the wind whistling through the canyons. His body nearly paralyzed with pain, he worked himself out of what remained of his Ranger. It was then that he saw the backseat. Amidst the mangled metal, Kailey's car seat was still strapped to the backseat, its tiny body harness still snapped in place. But Kailey had disappeared. Chris felt a sickening wave of panic. If she had been thrown from the truck during the fall she could not possibly be alive. She would have died immediately upon impact.

"Kailey!" he screamed, tears streaming down his face as he searched the steep hillside above him for his tiny daughter. Suddenly he knew what he had to do. He fell to his knees.

"Lord, thank you for allowing me to live through that fall." He whispered the words, his head hung in quiet desperation. "Now please, please let me find Kailey."

He stood up. "Kailey!" he yelled as loudly as he could, his voice choked by sobs. "If you can hear me, I'm coming to find you, sweetheart. Can you hear me, baby?"

Chris looked straight up at the rocky mountainside he would have to climb to reach the road. Suddenly, he saw people standing along the road's edge waving toward him. Then he remembered the cars that had been following him so closely. Someone must have seen the accident.

"Are you OK?" a man yelled, his voice echoing down the rocky canyon. Nearby, another passerby was already using a cellular telephone to call for help.

Fresh tears flooded his eyes as he screamed back, "Yes! But I can't find my daughter!"

Moving as quickly as possible, Chris began making his way up the hillside toward the people. He had begun coughing up blood, and his head felt as if it were about to explode. Still he continued to call Kailey's name every few feet. Finally, when he was forty feet from the road, he heard her.

"Daddy, Daddy," she cried. "I'm here!"

Chris felt a surge of hope and refused to give in to his body's desire to pass out. He had to reach her. "Kailey, I'm coming!" he shouted.

At that moment someone standing alongside the road pointed downward. "There she is!" Suddenly three of the bystanders were scrambling down the cliff toward a small clearing hidden from the road. They reached the child at about the same time Chris did. Kailey was sitting cross-legged on top of a soft, fern-fronded bush. Her eyes were black and blue, and she had dark purple bruises around her neck. She was shaking and crying hysterically. Instantly, Chris thought her neck must have been broken.

"Be careful of her neck," he shouted. "Let's lift her together."

"Yes," someone shouted from a few feet above the place where Kailey was sitting. "Let's get her up to the road."

Chris managed to stand beneath two men, helping to push his daughter up with his remaining strength as the others hoisted her to the highway. At about that time a medical helicopter landed on the highway twenty-five feet from the spot where Chris's truck had tumbled over the cliff. Paramedics began running toward Chris and Kailey, surrounding them and swiftly administering emergency aid. Within minutes, father and daughter were strapped to straight boards and air-lifted to Huntington Memorial Hospital in Pasadena.

Chris's head had swollen to nearly twice its normal size from the number of times it had slammed into the back of the truck. His lungs were also badly damaged from the pressure of his seat belt, which definitely saved his life. He was placed in intensive care and given a slim chance of survival.

Meanwhile, Kailey was taken to the pediatric unit where she was held for observation. Doctors took X-rays and determined that despite her severely bruised neck there was no damage to her spinal column. She had no internal injuries and had even escaped a concussion. Several hours passed before Michele got word of the accident and was able to rush to the hospital.

When she reached his side, Chris was unconscious, hooked up to numerous tubes and wires. His head was so swollen and his face so badly bruised that she hardly recognized him. She held his hand, crying and praying intently that he would survive. Then she went to find Kailey.

The little girl began crying when Michele hurried in, muffling a gasp at the sight of her bruised neck and eyes. Michele sat beside her quivering child and took her shivering body into her arms.

"It's OK, honey, everything's going to be all right," Michele murmured as she tried desperately to appear strong. "Why don't you tell me what happened?"

"Oh, Mommy," she cried harder, burying her head in her mother's embrace. After several seconds, Kailey finally looked up, tears streaming down her face and began to talk.

"We were driving and then we started to fall," she said, her eyes brimming with fresh tears. "Then the angels took me out and set me down on the bushes. But Daddy kept on rolling and rolling and rolling." Kailey began to cry harder. "I was so worried about him, I didn't know if he was ever going to stop rolling. Is he OK, Mommy?"

"He's going to be OK," Michele said, but she was trying to understand what Kailey had just said. "Sweetheart, tell me about the angels."

"They were nice. They took me out and set me on a soft bush."

Michele lay her daughter down gently on the pillow and ran her fingers over the purple bruises that circled her neck. Suddenly a chill ran the length of her spine and goose bumps popped up on her arms and legs. Angels? Taking Kailey from the car? She remembered scriptures that spoke about angels watching over those who love God.

"Do you know my angels, Mommy?" Kailey asked, no longer crying, her honest eyes filled with sincerity.

Michele shook her head. "No, Kailey, but I'm sure they did a good job getting you out of the truck. Sometimes God sends angels to take care of us."

Over the next few days, as Chris's condition began to miraculously improve, sheriff's investigations learned more about the accident. First, they determined that no one had ever survived a fall of 500 feet along the Angeles Crest Highway. Typically, even if a person is wearing a seat belt, the head injuries caused by rolling so many times cause fatal hemorrhaging.

Second, they found the Ranger's back window completely intact and only a few yards from the highway. Although they had never seen this happen before, the window had popped out in one piece upon initial impact with the steep embankment.

Next, they determined that Kailey would have had to fall out of the tumbling truck on the first roll for her to have landed where she did. Which meant that in a matter of seconds the back window must have popped out and Kailey must have somehow slipped through the straps of her seat belt and fallen backwards through the opening onto the soft bush.

"A virtual impossibility," the investigators later said. In addition, the area was covered with sharp, pointed yucca plants. Had she landed on one of them, the wide shoots that jut out from the plant could easily have punctured her small body and killed her. The soft bush where she was discovered was the only one of its kind in the immediate area.

"From all that we know about this accident," the investigators said later, "we will never know how Kailey Smith survived."

For Kailey, the explanation was obvious.

Months later, after Chris had made an astonishingly quick recovery and was home helping Michele with their newborn son and busy preparing the cabin for Christmas, Kailey continued to speak matter-of-factly of the angels who pulled her from Daddy's car, set her on the soft bush, and kept her safe until Daddy could reach her.

Left with no other explanation, Chris and Michele believe their daughter is telling the truth about what happened that August afternoon. About her very special encounter with angels.

Modern-Day Prodigal Son

∽

FROM THE HIGH STATION IN LIFE he has attained, Charles A. Galloway, Jr., can scarcely remember the rebellious teenager he was more than fifty years ago. Back then, in the winter of 1938, he had done things his way, regardless of his parents' deep concern for his life and future. During that time, an event took place that would change Charles's life forever.

The son of two loving and devoted parents, Charles had grown up in Jackson, Mississippi, and had been privileged with a wonderful childhood. But during his teenage years he had grown restless, anxious to experience a wilder lifestyle. At age sixteen he decided he no longer wanted to stay in school.

"Charles, I absolutely will not hear of you dropping out of school, you hear me?" his mother said when he presented her with the idea.

"But, Mom, I wanna be a prizefighter! I can do it, Mom. Give me a chance!"

"Nonsense," she said, turning away and shaking her head in disgust. "No son of mine is going to leave school for prizefighting."

His father agreed. "Stay in school, son. You don't have a choice."

The relationship with his parents became more and more strained. Charles waited until school was out for summer vacation and made plans to run away from home.

"I just need to be a man," he told one of his friends before he left. "Gotta set out on my own."

Charles was an intelligent boy, tall and athletic and with an innate sense of survival. Because he had only a few dollars, he knew he would first need to find work. After only one afternoon on his own, he discovered that by watching the railroad cars, he could determine approximately where they were headed.

He watched the station for nearly an hour. As with all train stops, this one was protected by railroad bulls, large club-bearing guards who kept people from stowing aboard the boxcars. When the trains began moving, the railroad bulls would climb aboard and ride near the front of the train. They were not worried about people stowing aboard while the train was moving, since to do so would have been foolishly dangerous. For that reason, it was rarely attempted.

Charles could imagine the dangers associated with jumping onto a moving train, but he was not afraid. He determined he would wait until the train was moving and take his chances. If his timing was right, he believed he could run alongside a slow-moving train and jump aboard one of the cargo cars without incident.

Summoning his courage, Charles waited for a train which appeared to be heading north out of Jackson and then made his move. If he missed, Charles knew he risked falling under the train's wheels. He forced himself to think positively, and at just the right moment, he jumped, landing safely inside the boxcar.

"Easier than it looks," Charles muttered confidently to himself.

He used his new mode of transportation several times over the next few days until he got off the train in a small Missouri town and saw what appeared to be a traveling carnival set up under a large banner that read "Red-Top Circus." His money spent, Charles approached the circus officials and was immediately hired as a roustabout.

"I'd also like to do a little fighting, if you don't mind," Charles added cockily, sticking out his chest as if to demonstrate his worthiness as a fighter.

The circus leader looked him over skeptically.

"We'll see, son," he said. "We just might be able to use you."

Now that he had found a place to stay and a way to make money, Charles wrote to his parents. They opened the letter together, tears of concern in their eyes.

"I can't tell you where I am, but I'm safe," he wrote in that first letter. "I may even get to do some prizefighting."

Over the next eight months, Charles traveled with the Red-Top Circus to dozens of towns from Missouri to Nebraska. Eventually, the circus leader allowed him to participate in the pit fights, in which two men were placed in a sunken pit and allowed to fight until one dropped from the punishing blows or from exhaustion. Charles didn't lose a single fight. Each time he won, he would go back to his sleeping quarters, pull out some paper and write a letter to his parents.

"I think you'd be proud of me," he would write. "Sure, I'm not in school. But I'm living out my dreams. Please don't worry about me."

Meanwhile, Charles's parents were naturally very worried about their son. They had always provided such a steady environment for him, and now he was a drifter, a roustabout and occasional fighter for a traveling circus. They handled their fears about his safety and his salvation by praying for him daily.

"Lord, please protect our son," they would pray aloud. "Keep him safe and bring him home."

In February, after a cold Nebraska winter took its toll on carnival attendance, the Red-Top Circus folded. Charles had enough money to take care of himself for quite some time. But he wanted to return to the south and knew his money would not pay for train fare. Resorting to his former method of travel, he stowed away on a series of trains until two weeks later he was in Hayti, Missouri. After a large lunch at a local diner, he considered his options. Returning home would be admitting failure. He really wanted to find another circus, somewhere he could resume fighting. That afternoon Charles scouted the area, only to discover that the nearest traveling circus was about twenty miles south. He knew just the train to take him south, and he hid himself near the railroad station's warehouse, under the loading dock. There he waited for the perfect moment. As he crouched in the shadows, he noticed that the train, which was still being loaded, would be pulled by two locomotives. That meant the train would pick up a great deal of speed much more quickly than usual. It might even be traveling close to full speed as it left the station. But he had jumped on fast-moving trains before and was not afraid.

When the time was right, he ran toward the boxcar and jogged alongside it. Suddenly, the ground beneath him narrowed and he was running alongside a steep ravine. A few feet ahead he could see that there was no land at all alongside the tracks—only a steep drop-off. Charles knew he had just one chance. Jumping before he had picked up the proper speed, he thrust himself upward and landed partially in the open boxcar. But with nothing to hold onto, his body began sliding out. As Charles struggled to pull himself inside the car, he could feel the train gaining full speed. Terrified at his predicament, he looked over his shoulder. The train was winding along the top of a very steep and narrow canyon ridge. If he slipped out he would either fall beneath the train's wheels or plummet down the steep canyon to his death. He closed his eyes and tried to will himself into the boxcar. Instead, he could feel himself slipping.

"Please, God!" he cried out, his eyes squeezed shut. "Don't let me die here." But Charles knew there was no way to survive the situation; he was seconds from certain death.

At that instant he opened his eyes. In front of him stood a fantastic-looking muscular black man in his thirties. The man was staring at him intently but said nothing; he only reached down and pulled the boy by his arms into the speeding boxcar. Charles lay facedown on the floor of the car for several seconds trying to catch his breath and regain his strength. When he looked up to thank the man, he had vanished. The boxcar was completely empty. One of the two side doors was closed, as it had been since the train began moving. He glanced outside and shuddered. There was no way the man could have jumped from the train and survived. He had simply disappeared from sight. Charles sat down slowly in a corner of the car and began shivering.

Suddenly he knew with great certainty that he needed to get home. He stayed on the train until it reached Jackson and immediately returned to his parents' home. He told them about the man on the boxcar.

"An angel, son," his father said, as his mother took them both in her arms. "God was watching out for you," she said. "See, he brought you home to us."

Charles nodded. "Things are going to be different now. You watch."

Charles returned to school that week and a few months later, his faith renewed, was baptized in the local river. After graduating, he moved to Southern California where he spent two years working as a professional prizefighter before being drafted. Charles served in World War II with the 339th Bomb Squadron in the 96th Bomb Group of the Eighth Air Force. He flew twenty-eight combat missions over Germany, and in May 1945, he returned to Jackson and went into the construction business with his father. Working together, their business became both lucrative and well-respected.

Now, at age seventy-one, Charles shares his story with anyone whose faith needs reaffirming. He is convinced that God saved his life by sending a guardian angel to get his attention.

"My entire life would be different if it weren't for that single afternoon," says Charles, whose faith and love for God is always evident these days. "God used that angel not only to save my life but to change it into something that could glorify him forever."

A Stranger of Light
in the Cancer Ward

ᴥ

HE BAD NEWS CAME JANUARY 6, 1981.

Until then, Melissa and Chris Deal were by most standards one of the happiest couples anywhere. They were in their early twenties, lived in Nashville, Tennessee, and shared a passion for country music and the outdoors. They were constantly finding new ways to enjoy each other's company, whether by mountain-biking, hiking, or playing tennis together. Attractive and athletic, Melissa and Chris seemed to live a charmed life in which everything went their way.

That was before Chris got sick. At first the couple believed he was only suffering from a severe cold. Then they wondered if perhaps he had contracted mononucleosis. But the doctors chose to run blood tests; and finally, on that cold January day, Chris's condition was diagnosed as acute lymphatic leukemia. At age 28, Chris was suffering with the deadliest form of childhood cancer.

During the next three months, Chris's cancer slipped into remission and he stayed the picture of health. Muscular at six feet two inches and two hundred pounds, Chris looked more like a professional athlete than a man suffering from leukemia. During that time, Chris continued to work, and neither he nor Melissa spent much time talking about his illness.

At the end of that period, doctors discovered that Chris's brother was a perfect match for a bone marrow transplant. But before the operation could be scheduled, Chris's remission ended dramatically and he became very ill.

"I'm afraid he's too weak to undergo a transplant," Chris's doctor explained as the couple sat in his office one afternoon. "The cancer has become very aggressive."

The doctor recommended that Chris be admitted to Houston's cancer hospital, M.D. Anderson, for continuous treatment in hopes of forcing the disease into remission. Within a week, Chris and Melissa had taken medical leaves of absence from their jobs and both moved into the Houston hospital. The nurses generously set up a cot for Melissa so that she could stay beside Chris, encouraging him and furnishing him strength during his intensive chemotherapy and radiation treatments.

Living in a cancer ward was very depressing for the Deals, who had previously seen very little of death and dying. The couple talked often about how their lives had become little more than a nightmare in which Chris fought for his life amidst other people like him, people with no real chance of overcoming their cancer. Chris began to spend a great deal of time in prayer, asking God to take care of Melissa no matter what happened to him. He prayed for remission, but also asked God for the strength to accept his death if his time had come to die.

Months passed and doctors began to doubt whether Chris's cancer would ever be in remission again. By Christmas, 1981, Chris weighed only one hundred pounds. His eyes were sunken into his skull, and he had lost nearly all of his strength. He was no longer able to walk and only rarely found the energy needed to sit up in bed. Doctors told Melissa that there was nothing more they could do.

"I don't think he has much longer, Melissa," one doctor said. "I want you to be ready."

Melissa nodded, tears streaming down her cheeks. She felt completely alone and wondered how their happy life together had turned so tragic. She began to fear that Chris would die while she slept, and for that reason she dozed for only an hour or so at a time, waking quickly each time Chris moved or tried to speak.

On January 4, Melissa fell into a deeper sleep than usual and was awakened at 3 a.m. by a nurse.

"Mrs. Deal," the nurse said, her voice urgent, "wake up! Your husband has gone."

Thinking that her husband had died in his sleep, Melissa sat straight up, afraid of what she might see. But Chris's hospital bed was empty.

"He's gone! Where is he, what happened? Where did you take him?" she asked frantically.

"We haven't moved him, ma'am," the nurse said quickly. "He must have gotten up and walked somewhere. We came in to check his vital signs and he was gone."

Melissa shook her head, willing herself to think clearly. "He can't walk. You know that." She was frustrated and her voice rose a level.

Even if her husband had found the strength to get out of bed and shuffle into the hallway, he would have been seen. Chris's room was on the circular eleventh floor of the cancer hospital, and the nurses' station was a round island in the center of the floor. There was no way Chris could have gotten up and walked out of his room without someone spotting him. Especially since each of his arms was attached to intravenous tubing.

The nurse appeared flustered and shaken, and suddenly Melissa jumped to her feet and ran from the room. As she ran toward the elevators, Melissa's eyes caught a slight movement in the eleventh-floor chapel. Heading for the door and peering inside, Melissa was stunned by what she saw.

Inside the chapel, with his back to the door, Chris was sitting casually in one of the pews and talking with a man. He was unfettered by intravenous tubing, and although still very thin, he appeared to be almost healthy.

Melissa was filled with anger. Why had Chris left without saying anything? And who was this man? Melissa knew she had never seen him before, and he wasn't dressed like a doctor. Where had he come from at three in the morning? Melissa stared through the window trying to make sense of what was happening.

After several minutes passed, Melissa walked into the chapel toward her husband. At the same time, the stranger looked down at the floor, almost as if he did not want Melissa to see his face. She noted that he was dressed in a red-checked flannel work shirt, blue jeans, and a brand new pair of lace-up work boots. His white hair was cut short to his head, and his skin was so white it appeared transparent. Melissa turned toward Chris, still keeping one eye on the man across from him.

"Chris?" she said, questioningly. "Are you all right? Where have you been?"

"Melissa, it's OK," Chris said, laughing casually and appearing stronger than he had in months. "I'll be back in the room in a little while."

At that instant, she turned toward the stranger and he looked up at her. Melissa was struck by the brilliance of his clear blue eyes. Who was he? she wondered. How was he able to make Chris laugh and appear so at ease when only hours earlier he had been barely able to move? Melissa stared at the man, mesmerized by the look in his eyes and searching for an explanation as to his existence.

"What's going on?" she asked, turning back toward her husband.

"Melissa, please, I'll be back in the room soon!" Chris's voice was gentle but adamant. Melissa knew that he wanted her to leave them alone.

Reluctantly, Melissa turned to go, making her way back to the center station where she informed Chris's nurses that he was in the chapel. They were relieved and did not attempt to bring him back to his room.

For thirty minutes, Melissa waited alone in the hospital room until finally Chris joined her. Melissa almost didn't recognize him. With a wide grin on his face and a twinkle in his eyes, Chris appeared to be full of energy as he walked toward her with a strength he hadn't had before. He was obviously happy and at peace with himself.

"OK, I want to know who that man was. Why were you talking to him? What did he say? And how come you're walking so well? What happened?" Melissa fired the questions at her husband in succession and he began laughing.

"Melissa, he was an angel."

His happiness and the way Chris spoke those words left no doubt in Melissa's mind that he believed what he had said was the truth. She was silent a moment, allowing herself to ponder the possibility that the man had indeed been an angel.

"I believe you," she said softly, reaching toward her husband and taking his hand in hers. "Tell me about it."

Chris told her that he had been jerked awake and instantly experienced an overpowering urge to go to the chapel. His tubing had already been removed, something none of the nurses remembered doing when they were asked later. As he moved to climb out of bed and begin walking, he was suddenly able to do so without any of his usual weakness. When he got to the chapel, he quietly moved into a pew and kneeled to pray. He was praying silently when he heard a voice.

"Are you Chris Deal?" the voice asked gently.

"Yes," Chris answered, curiously unafraid of the voice.

At that instant, he turned around and the man was there, dressed in a flannel shirt and jeans. The man sat directly across from Chris, their knees almost touching. For a moment the man said nothing. When he spoke, Chris had the feeling he already knew the man.

"Do you need forgiveness for anything?" the man asked.

Chris hung his head, his eyes welling up with tears. For years he had held bitter and resentful feelings toward a relative he'd known most of his life. He had always known it was wrong to harbor such hatred, but he had never asked for forgiveness. Slowly, Chris looked up and nodded, explaining the situation to the man.

The man told Chris that God had forgiven him. "What else is bothering you?"

"Melissa. My wife," Chris said, the concern showing on his face. "I'm worried about her. What's going to happen to her?"

The man smiled peacefully. "She will be fine."

The man knelt alongside Chris, and for the next twenty minutes the two men prayed together. Finally, the man turned toward Chris and smiled.

"Your prayers have been answered, Chris. You can go now."

Chris thanked the man, and although nothing had been said he somehow was certain the man was an angel.

"And then I came back here," Chris said cheerfully.

Suddenly Melissa leapt to her feet. "I have to find him," she said as she left the room.

Melissa believed Chris's story but she was overwhelmed with the need to talk to the man herself. She ran back to the chapel but the man was gone. Next, she checked the guards who were at their post at each elevator. She described the man Chris had talked with.

"A man in a flannel shirt and jeans," the guard repeated curiously. "No, haven't seen anyone like that."

Melissa hurried into the elevator and traveled to the first floor. The guards at the hospital's main entrance had also not seen anyone who fit the man's description.

"But that's impossible," Melissa insisted. "I know he had to have gone through these doors less than fifteen minutes ago. He couldn't have just disappeared."

"Sorry, ma'am," the guard said. "I haven't seen anyone like that all night."

Feeling defeated, Melissa returned to Chris's hospital room where he was sitting, his arms crossed in front of him, with a knowing look on his face.

"Didn't find him, right?" Chris said, grinning.

"Where did he go? I really want to talk to him." Melissa was frustrated, baffled by the man's sudden disappearance.

"I guess he went to wherever he came from, honey. He did what he came to do and he left."

Slowly, Melissa nodded as if she understood. She still wished she had been able to find the man, but apparently Chris was right. The man had completely disappeared, perhaps to return to wherever he had come from.

The next day when Chris awoke, even more energetic than he had been the night before, both Melissa and Chris thought he was miraculously in remission. He was happy and content and spent much of the day visiting the other patients on the floor and offering them encouragement by praying with them or merely listening to them. Many physical manifestations of his illness seemed to have lessened or disappeared as mysteriously as the man who had visited him.

Then, two days later, Melissa awoke to find Chris staring at her strangely. Suddenly nervous, Melissa sat up in bed. "What?" she asked.

"I dreamed about Bill last night," Chris said, clearly confused by the dream. "You told me to tell you if I ever dreamed about Bill."

Bill, Chris's best friend, had died in a car accident the year before. For reasons that were unclear to her, Melissa believed that if Chris ever dreamed about Bill, it meant Chris's death was imminent. She hadn't told Chris these thoughts but had asked him to tell her if he ever dreamed about Bill.

Now Melissa was confused. Chris couldn't be near death. He looked vibrant and strong. And if his prayers had been answered, as the flannel-shirted man had told him, then he must have been on his way to recovery. Something wasn't making sense.

"What about the angel?" she asked Chris, her voice filled with anxiety.

Chris shrugged. "I don't know. You just asked me to tell you if I ever dreamed about Bill." Something in Chris's face told Melissa he knew why she had considered the dream significant.

That afternoon, Chris suffered a pulmonary hemorrhage. He began bleeding from his mouth and nose, and immediately there were dozens of doctors and medical experts swarming around, desperately trying to save his life. Melissa moved to a place behind Chris's head and placed her hands on his shoulders.

"Come on, Chris," she shouted frantically. "Stay with me!" At that moment one of the doctors asked her to step aside so they could work on him.

Melissa backed up slowly and found a spot in the room against the wall where she sank down to the floor and buried her head in her hands.

While the doctors hurried about Chris, shouting "Code Blue" and trying to save his life, she began to pray. Almost instantly, she felt a peace wash over her and realized that this was part of God's plan. Chris had prayed that she would be all right, and at that instant she knew she would be, no matter what happened.

That afternoon, minutes before he was pronounced dead, exactly one year after being diagnosed with cancer, Chris called out Melissa's name.

"It's OK, honey," she whispered, her tear-covered face gazing upward. "It's OK."

Now, more than ten years later, Melissa believes that Chris's prayers had indeed been answered that night when he was visited by the man she believes was an angel. Since his time on earth was running short, he had been given the gift of peace, of accepting his fate and not fighting it in fear. Also, he had been released from the bondage of bitterness and hatred and graced with the gift of God's forgiveness. That fact was evident in the happiness and contentment of his final days. And finally, Melissa had survived Chris's death and came out stronger for the ordeal—another answer to Chris's prayer.

Although there are people who might try to explain or argue about the identity of Chris's visitor that night, Melissa saw him, looked him in the eyes and watched the transformation his visit made in Chris's life. As far as she's concerned, there will never be any explanation other than the one Chris gave her that same night: "Melissa, he was an angel."

Priority Check

OANNE DAVIS HAD NEVER BEEN ONE to put stock in material wealth. Even when she strayed from her religious roots as a young, independent college student, she cared little about the brand of clothes she wore or the make of car she drove.

Instead of things, people were the focus of JoAnne's life. When those around her were hurting, she felt their pain. When they needed a hand up or a handout, she provided it whenever possible.

When JoAnne turned thirty-two in the spring of 1993, through a series of unexpected circumstances, JoAnne wound up the owner of a brand-new yellow Cadillac sedan. By then she had found her way through prayer back to a strong relationship with God and believed that the car was a gift from Him. God had trusted her with such a car, she figured, because she did not hold great admiration for luxury items—thus, it would not interfere with her life in any way.

Still, the car was far different from the old practical vehicles she had driven in the past, and she enjoyed being able to take friends places in style. She was not surprised that she was enjoying the car. What surprised her was the way in which God chose to test her priorities not long after she received the Cadillac.

It was a particularly warm day in June, and JoAnne had picked up her friend B.B. for a trip to the local shopping mall. The women were chatting casually when, just before they pulled into the mall's parking lot, JoAnne spied a man limping along the sidewalk. He seemed to be in his 60s, and he wore black slacks, a dress shirt and a tie—all of them tattered and torn. As JoAnne drove past him, she saw that sweat was pouring down his face as he struggled to move forward.

Then she glanced down and saw the reason for his struggle. Although he walked without the aid of a cane, the man's right foot was deformed, turning in severely at the ankle and forcing the man to bear weight on the ankle bone with each step.

"I can't believe that," JoAnne gasped, instantly aching for the man.

B.B. turned to see what had caught her friend's attention and sized up the man's situation. "How sad," she said.

Caught in the flow of traffic, JoAnne turned right into the parking lot, drove up one aisle and down another, parked her new car, and turned off the engine. From her vantage point, she could see that the man was still making painstaking progress along the sidewalk and suddenly she could no longer stand to watch.

"That's it," she said, starting the engine up once again.

"What?" B.B. asked, her hand on the door handle.

"I can't stand it. That man's suffering," JoAnne explained, pulling the car back into the aisle. She headed for the same area where she had entered the mall moments earlier. The man reached the spot just as she did, and JoAnne leaned out of her car window.

"Sir, can I give you a ride somewhere?" she said, loud enough that the man looked up and smiled at her.

"Why, that would be very kind of you," he said. "I missed my bus and I need to get back to my apartment. It's only a mile from here."

Ignoring the traffic that had begun to build up behind her, JoAnne climbed out of her car, opened her back door, and helped the man inside. Now that he was so close, JoAnne was nearly overcome by the stench from the man's filthy clothes. She glanced at the backseat of her new car. But almost at the same time she reminded herself that she had done nothing to earn the car. It had been a gift from God, in her opinion, and if she could use it to help a struggling human being, she would do so gladly.

As she got back into the driver's seat and pulled out onto the road, she asked the man exactly where he needed to go. Glancing in the rearview mirror, she noticed his strange hair color. For his age, the man's strawberry blond hair seemed unnatural. Also, he seemed utterly peaceful and unaffected by his condition. Whereas before he had been struggling so intensely, now he seemed rested and without a care.

JoAnne wrinkled her eyebrows in curiosity and struck up a conversation with the man. She talked about how she and her friend were going to attend a church program that night and how the choir had been working on it for weeks. When the man remained silent, JoAnne tried another approach to get him talking.

"Do you know the Lord?" she asked simply.

The man looked up suddenly and then seemed almost flustered. "Oh, well, that's another matter," he said quickly and then immediately pointed up the street at the apartment building where he wanted to be dropped off.

JoAnne considered his answer and thought there was practically nothing she could say in response. She cast a questioning glance toward B.B. who, also puzzled by the man's words, shrugged her shoulders.

"Here," he said, breaking the silence. "Right here. Thank you so much." He waited until JoAnne had pulled up to the curb, and then he began to open the door. She quickly got out and helped him up onto the curb. Then she took a piece of paper from her purse and scribbled her phone number.

"Here," she said, handing the paper to the elderly man. "If you ever need a ride or anything at all, please give me a call. I'd like to help."

As the man took the paper, he looked intently at JoAnne and smiled. "God bless you," he said softly. Then he backed up a few steps and watched as JoAnne returned to her car and prepared to leave.

But just as she was about to pull away from the curb, JoAnne suddenly wondered if the man did indeed live in the apartments. After all, he was still standing with his back to the entrance. Perhaps he was homeless and didn't have any place to go. Although troubled by these thoughts, JoAnne pulled back into traffic and began driving.

After passing two other buildings, she stopped abruptly and turned the car back to the apartment where she had dropped off the man. She had to know if he really had a home or if now he would be all alone again.

But as soon as she made the turn, she peered toward the sidewalk where the man had been standing seconds earlier and realized that he had vanished. She sped up and pulled up against the curb once more. The apartment entrance consisted of a long corridor with no doors opening off of it. JoAnne stared up the corridor but there was no one in sight.

"Where is he?" B.B. exclaimed, astonished that the man had disappeared.

"I don't know, but come on." JoAnne climbed out of the car and began trotting toward the building. "He's got to be here somewhere."

For ten minutes the friends searched the perimeter of the building, the bushes that ran along the front of it and up and down the street. The man was nowhere to be found.

Finally, they gave up and returned to JoAnne's car. They sat in the car and discussed the impossibility of what had happened. They had seen how slowly the man walked. His handicap would have prevented him from walking more than ten or fifteen feet in the time it took JoAnne to turn around and come back.

Suddenly, B.B. gasped. "JoAnne! What if the man was an angel?"

JoAnne leaned back against her seat and stared ahead pensively. She had always tried to help people in the past, had hurt for them sometimes more than they hurt for themselves. But then she had received the Cadillac.

"You mean like a test or something?" she asked, turning toward her friend.

B.B. nodded. "Would you still be willing to help people even if it meant opening your new car to a smelly, dirty, dejected man like him."

JoAnne thought a moment and then smiled. "There's really no other explanation, is there?"

"Not really."

"I guess I never thought God's angels looked like *that*," JoAnne said. "But it makes sense. Especially if it's a test of some kind."

"Well, if it was a test I'd say you passed with flying colors. What is it the Bible says about angels and being kind to them?"

JoAnne glanced around one last time and then started the car. She smiled and turned to her friend. "Be careful to entertain strangers. For in doing so, some have entertained angels without knowing it."

The Littlest Angel

ॐ

OUGLAS TANNER WAS EXHAUSTED. After fifteen years of neurological work in Boston, he had developed an extensive list of patients and an equally impressive reputation. But Tanner paid the price for his success, especially on days like this.

The hospital had been overcrowded, probably because of the cold, wintry weather that January 1957, and the accompanying increase in illnesses. In addition to helping tend to the swarms of people who seemed to line the halls of every floor of the hospital, Tanner had been busier than usual, with exceptionally burdensome work: several examinations and two tiring surgeries.

Tanner peeled off his navy cardigan sweater and shuffled into the kitchen where his wife, Cheri, sat at their kitchen table reading a women's magazine.

"Long day?" she asked with a gentle smile, rising to receive his embrace.

"Hmmm." Tanner needed no words for moments like this. Cheri had been a part of his life since his days in medical school, and she knew by the look on his face what type of day he'd had. He sat down slowly, stretching out his legs and enjoying the sensation of muscles relaxing throughout his body. At forty-two years old, he was in very good shape and usually looked ten years younger. Today he looked his age and more.

"Dinner's in the refrigerator," Cheri said, tilting her head and waiting for his response.

"Maybe later. Right now I only need you and this wonderful old chair."

Suddenly, they heard someone run up their front steps and ring the doorbell. Tanner and his wife exchanged a puzzled look. It was nearly nine o'clock, bitterly cold, and snow had been piling up outside for the past two hours.

Tanner stood up and released a long sigh. "Who in the world could that be at this hour?" He headed toward the front room.

"Yes?" he said as he opened the door.

There, shivering on their doorstep, stood a little girl dressed in torn rags, a tattered coat, and worn-out shoes. Tanner guessed she couldn't have been more than five years old. She was crying and she turned her huge brown eyes up toward Tanner's.

"Sir, my mother is dying," she said, her voice choked by the sobs. Tanner felt his entire insides melting with concern for the child. She had the sweetest, purest voice he'd ever heard. "Please could you come? We don't live far."

Tanner did not hesitate. He turned quickly back toward Cheri, who waited behind him. "Get my sweater and overcoat, dear. I'll be back soon as I can."

Cheri smiled as she retrieved the items and watched her husband bundle up. Her husband had chosen the medical field because he enjoyed helping people. Now, with someone's life in jeopardy, he would not remember how tired he had been until he was home and the woman safely cared for.

Tanner took the little girl's hand and the two headed out the door and into the storm. Less than two city blocks away, in a section of tenement apartments, the little girl turned into a doorway and led Tanner up two flights of stairs.

"She's in there," the little girl said, pointing toward a bedroom at the end of a narrow hallway.

Tanner moved quickly toward the bedroom and found a woman who was very sick, fever racking her thin body. She was nearly delirious, her eyes closed as she writhed under the blankets, moaning unintelligibly. Tanner determined immediately that she was suffering from pneumonia and that he would need to bring her fever down if there was any chance to save her life. For more than an hour he worked over the woman, soothing her hot, dry skin with compresses and arranging for her to be transported to the nearest medical facility.

Finally, when her fever began to subside, the woman opened her eyes slowly, blinking because of the bright light. She saw the doctor, still working tirelessly to cool her body with wet rags, and she thanked him for coming.

"How did you ever find me?" she asked shyly. "I have been sick for so long I might have died without your help. How can I ever thank you?"

Tanner smiled. "Your little girl saved your life. I would never have known you were up here otherwise. Thank her. Sweet little child, braving a cold, stormy night like this and walking the streets until she found me. She must have been awfully worried about you."

A look of pain and shock filled the woman's eyes. "What are you talking about?" she asked, her voice dropping to little more than a baffled whisper.

Tanner was puzzled. "Your little girl," he repeated. "She came and got me. That's how I found you here."

The woman began shaking her head and her hand flew to her mouth as if she were trying to stop herself from screaming out loud.

"What is it, what's wrong?" Tanner took the woman's hand in his and tried to soothe her sudden panic. "Your little girl's all right."

"Sir..." Tears were streaming down the woman's face as she was finally able to drum up the strength to speak. "My little girl died a month ago. She was sick for weeks and..." She paused a moment, bending her head and allowing the sobs to come.

Tanner stepped back, shocked by the woman's story. "But she knocked on my door and led me here! I held her hand until she showed me where you were."

The woman's tears were coming harder now and she pointed toward a closet in her cramped bedroom. "There," she said between sobs. "That's where I keep her things since she died."

Tanner walked slowly toward the closet, almost aware of what he might see before he actually saw it. He opened the door gingerly and there they were. The coat worn by the little girl only an hour earlier hung completely dry in the closet. The girl's tattered shoes sat neatly on the floor of the closet.

"These belonged to your daughter?" he asked, turning toward the woman.

"Yes, sir," she said, wiping her wet cheeks with the sleeve from her nightgown.

Tanner turned back toward the tiny coat and shoes. "The girl who led me here wore this coat and those shoes," he said, almost as if he were talking to himself.

Suddenly he turned and ran toward the room where he had last seen the little girl. When he could not find her, he hurried throughout the apartment from one room to the next. The little girl had disappeared. After he had finished his search he returned to the girl's mother.

"She's gone," he said flatly.

The woman nodded and suddenly her face broke into a smile, the tears replaced by a strange peaceful look. "Her angel has come back to help me. How else do you explain this?"

Tanner shook his head slowly. He had no answers for the woman. He walked home slowly that night, pondering the impossible and wondering about life. He had been gifted with the knowledge of medicine, a knowledge that often meant the difference between life and death in a patient. Yet, there was so much he did not know, so much he would never understand in this life.

Years later, he would tell the story about the littlest child who, although dead more than a month, had somehow summoned him from his home to help her dying mother. And he would still feel the same sense of amazement he had that cold, wintry evening. Although there was no earthly explanation for what had happened that night in Boston, he believed in his heart that the woman had been right. The girl must have been an angel. The littlest one of all.

An Angelic Reminder

HEN HER MOTHER PRESENTED HER WITH THE IDEA, Amber Cook was anything but excited.

"Texas!" the nineteen-year-old minister's daughter shouted in exasperation. She had grown up in Southern California and enjoyed the beaches and sunshine and city atmosphere where she lived in Fullerton. "I hate Texas. There's no way I'm going to Texas."

The plan, her mother explained, was for Amber to meet up with one of their church friends in Texas where she would join an eight-member Christian singing group called Departure, which would travel the country visiting churches for one year.

"It'll be good for you, Amber," her mother said confidently. "I want you to at least think about it. You know you've been looking for a way to get out of town for a while."

A beautiful blonde with brown eyes and a singing voice that easily rivaled any of the professional recording artists, Amber was currently having trouble getting a former boyfriend to stop calling. Because of that, when Amber's mother heard about the offer, she thought the trip would give Amber the desired separation from the young man.

Amber shuddered at the thought of spending a year in small towns across the country. She had lived in Southern California since junior high and knew how much she would miss her friends. But Amber also loved to sing. She had dazzled local audiences since she was four years old and had occasionally been approached by talent agents. She had even developed a fanlike following among the large congregation where her father was minister. Someday, Amber always told herself, she would pursue a professional singing career. And though she was not quite ready to make that career move, the idea of singing nearly every night for a year was enticing. Finally, her desire to share her faith through song became stronger than her dislike for small towns. She agreed to fly to Texas and spend a week with Frank and Ruth, her mother's friends from church, and the other members of Departure.

At week's end, despite the lack of city luxuries, Amber was hooked. She flew home, spent a week packing and bidding her family and friends farewell, and then flew to meet the group in Baton Rouge, Louisiana. The group traveled from one city to the next in Frank and Ruth's motor home. Each night they would sing at a different church, hoping to soften the hearts of those in attendance. Typically, when the performance was over, they would collect small donations that would pay their food and gasoline costs until they reached their next destination.

For the first few weeks, Amber experienced an indescribable joy when she sang about Jesus to a churchful of people. There were many ways to tell a person about God's love, and her way was song. She felt as if God had a purpose for her life, and she could hardly wait for the concerts each night.

But as time passed, the joy of singing began to wear thin in light of the group's circumstances. Amber suddenly found herself focusing instead on the inconvenience of sharing a motor home with seven other people. There were occasional tire blowouts and breakdowns and times when the group's funds ran so low, there was no telling where their next meal would come from. In addition, Frank had a heart that was, in Amber's opinion, far too generous. If a needy person crossed their path, Frank would use their dinner money to buy him or her a sandwich, always believing easily that God would somehow provide their means. Even though they had never gone without, Amber was still bothered by Frank's total selflessness.

One afternoon, three months into the tour, the group stopped at a small southern seaside town for an Italian dinner. Weeks had passed since they had eaten anything other than fast food, but the previous night's offering had brought in enough that Frank decided they could afford a sit-down dinner.

As the group approached the restaurant, they noticed a man dressed in tattered rags with dirt covering his face and matted hair.

"Bum!" Amber whispered to herself in disgust. "Watch Frank invite him to dinner."

As the group drew closer to the man, Amber was horrified when Frank stopped and started up a conversation with him. Amber got closer so she could hear what they were saying, and suddenly she was assaulted by the man's body odor and the smell of musty alcohol on his breath. Stepping away, Amber guessed that months had passed since the man's last bath. Disgusting, she thought to herself. The man has no pride in himself whatsoever!

Through their conversation, Frank learned that the man was homeless. He had been on the streets for the past year and needed some money for food. Frank smiled. There was only one way to be certain the man used the money for food.

"I can't give you any money," he said gently. "But we'd love to have you eat dinner with us. Our treat."

The homeless man looked skeptical. "You wanna bring me the food out here?" he asked, refusing to believe that Frank might actually want such a man eating with his group.

"No, of course not!" Frank said, waving toward the restaurant door, where the manager was watching them in conversation. "Come in! Eat with us."

The man stared at the members of the group, his eyes resting on Amber. Then he shrugged and stood up.

"What's your name?" Frank asked as they moved inside.

"Gus."

Amber dropped toward the back of the group and rolled her eyes in frustration. Now they'd have to smell this filthy man for the next hour and no one would enjoy the meal. She shook her head and followed the others into the restaurant. The tour really wasn't working out like she'd hoped.

Once inside, the manager showed them to a table near the back of a large, square-shaped room. Amber sat down first and waited for the others to fill in beside her. When everyone had found a seat Amber was horrified to see that the seat beside her was still empty. The homeless man still stood off to the side, unsure of whether he should really join the group at a formal dinner table. He looked embarrassed as he scanned his ragged and torn clothing.

"I'll just go outside and wait," he said suddenly. "You can bring me something out there if you want."

Frank stood up and shook his head. "Absolutely not," he said, pointing to the seat beside Amber. "Sit right there."

Amber slid as far away from the empty seat as she could and prayed she wouldn't lose her appetite. She already felt suffocated by the man's putrid smell.

Just ignore him, she told herself, determined to enjoy her meal despite the man's presence.

After the group placed their order, the man looked at Frank and began to speak.

"Where are you people from?" he asked, making eye contact around the table.

Frank cleared his voice. "We're just a traveling Christian singing group. Call ourselves Departure," he told the man. Amber pretended to be studying her silverware. If they were really a traveling singing group they would certainly have a more luxurious set of circumstances than these, she told herself wryly.

"Christians, huh?" Gus asked doubtfully. "Well, Christians, I have a few questions for you." The man waited until everyone, even Amber, was watching him attentively. "You people are always talking about how much God loves me. How am I supposed to believe that? Look at me, living on the streets. If God loves me why doesn't he get me off the streets?"

Frank looked around the group waiting to see if anyone wanted to answer the question. When everyone remained silent, he turned toward Gus.

"Well, Gus, God's love doesn't really show up in fine clothes and comfortable lifestyles," he began. "But I can prove God loves you."

The man raised an eyebrow and grunted. "OK, prove it."

"Have you heard about Jesus?"

The man nodded.

"Jesus died for you, Gus, did you know that?" Frank asked.

"I've heard about that, but I guess it never really made much difference to me."

At that moment, Ruth began to speak. "If there hadn't been anyone else in the world, Jesus still would have died for you. He loves you that much," she said softly. "Of course it's up to you, whether you want to believe He's who He says He is. We all have the right to refuse His gift of eternal life."

Two of the other group members nodded in unison. "You know why He died, right?" one of them asked.

Gus shook his head. "Not really."

As the conversation progressed, Amber forgot the man's dirty condition and became deeply interested. Having been raised in a Christian home, she had never been around anyone who knew as little about God as this man apparently did. She took for granted that everyone had been exposed to the same type of upbringing she'd been given. She turned in her chair so she could get a better look at him.

"Jesus died to pay the price for our sins," Frank said simply. "Basically, because of Him you're a free man, Gus."

"A free man? I've always been free."

"Not really," Amber cut in, and the others looked at her in surprise. Then she turned toward Gus again. "When we're free in Christ, our circumstances don't really matter any more. All that matters is He is with us, He loves us, and He'll see us safely home in the end."

As Amber finished speaking, her words hit with a dramatic force. For weeks she had been complaining about the cramped quarters in the motor home and the other inconveniences of living on the road. Amidst her grumbling and complaining, she had forgotten the reason she had agreed to be part of the group. She hadn't chosen this lifestyle because of the comfortable surroundings or so that she could receive special treatment from others. Her purpose was only to tell people about Jesus. Now, this man sat beside her, hungry for the truth of a message she had understood since childhood. A wave of humility came over Amber, and she silently asked God's forgiveness for passing judgment on the man.

For the next thirty minutes the group shared with Gus stories from their lives, testimonies detailing how they knew for certain that God was near them. Finally, the man seemed to understand. He even wore a different look, as if there was hope in his life when only an hour earlier there had been none.

"Come with us," Frank said as the group prepared to leave. "We'll take you to the next town. There's a big church there and we'll set you up with someone who can help you."

Gus nodded absently, glancing at a clock on the wall. "Need to get to the bathroom first," he said, standing up and moving quickly toward the front entrance of the restaurant.

Frank and the others watched him go, and after less than a minute had passed, Frank stood up. "I'm going to make sure he's all right. He might need some help."

The others got up at the same time and agreed to meet Frank and Gus outside the restaurant entrance. After several minutes, Frank walked outside, wearing a baffled expression.

"I can't find him anywhere," he said. "He's not in the bathroom, and I asked the cooks. He hasn't been back to the kitchen, either. He didn't walk out this way, did he?"

The group members scanned the length of the street and shook their heads. "Haven't seen him," one member said.

Frank walked back into the restaurant and went up to the manager, whose desk was just inside the doorway.

"Have you seen a man with sort of old, ripped clothes and..."

"Oh, you mean the bum you brought in to eat with you?" the manager asked.

"Yes, did he walk out this way?"

"No. I've been here for the past half hour and he hasn't come this way."

Frank walked slowly outside, shaking his head. There were only three ways out of the restaurant—through the emergency fire door, which would have sounded a loud siren if it had been opened; through the kitchen loading door; and through the front entrance. No one had seen Gus near any of those exits.

"I can't understand it. It's like he just disappeared," Frank said, still scanning the restaurant hallway and looking out the front doorway up and down the sidewalk.

At that moment, Amber felt that she knew the truth. "You don't think, maybe..." she began and then grew silent. Her father had been a minister for years and believed in every truth the Bible taught. Because of that, there had been times when he talked about angels in his sermons.

"They're real," he had told his children one day. "Because God says they're real."

Frank looked at her a moment and then understood. "You mean, maybe he was an angel?"

Amber nodded.

Frank looked down the street again, searching for some sign of the man. "I guess we'll never know."

But suddenly Amber was convinced that God had sent the man to remind her of her purpose—not just her purpose while traveling with Departure, but her purpose in life. Today, whenever she sees someone less fortunate than she is, she remembers Gus and a Bible verse from Hebrews:

"Do not forget to entertain strangers, for by doing so some people have entertained angels without knowing it."

Badge-Bearing Angel

OSHUA JONES WAS TRYING DESPERATELY TO STAY AWAKE. He had been the keynote speaker at a retreat in the mountains near Flagstaff, Arizona, and now, at 11:30 p.m., was driving the remote stretches of Interstate 17 back to Phoenix. It was very warm, and his car's air conditioning had stopped working earlier in the week. The warm air and solitary highway were causing Joshua to nod off occasionally, and he was finding it nearly impossible to concentrate on his driving.

"Come on, Lord," he prayed aloud, his voice urgent. "Keep me awake. Just until the next rest stop."

Less than a minute later, Joshua saw flashing lights in his rearview mirror. There had been almost no traffic on the interstate for miles, and the area he was traveling was utterly remote. Joshua, who had been driving barefoot, struggled to put his shoes on as he pulled his car over, briefly wondering what a police officer was doing in this area. One thing was certain; he was definitely wide awake now that an officer was pulling him over.

He stopped his car on the shoulder of the road, his shoes now on his feet, and watched in his mirror as the officer approached the car. He wore a standard highway patrol uniform but he was smiling. Joshua had only received two tickets in his life, none of them from smiling officers.

"Good evening, officer," Joshua said as the patrolman stopped beside his open window.

"Are you alright?" he asked, bending over a bit and looking at Joshua with searching eyes. Joshua noted his badge number: 37.

"Yes, fine."

The officer laughed. "At least you have your shoes on now."

Joshua looked puzzled. How had the officer known about his shoes? Before he could voice the question, the officer spoke again.

"You've been driving a long way and it's late. You almost fell asleep out there, didn't you?"

"Why, yes," Joshua stammered. "I was really struggling to stay awake. Maybe you can tell me where the nearest rest stop is."

"Better yet, I'll take you there," the officer said. "You spent the weekend helping everyone else, now it's your turn to get a little assistance. Follow me." The officer turned to leave.

"Wait!" Joshua cried. "Aren't you giving me a ticket or something?"

The officer looked at him evenly and shook his head. "No ticket. Just wanted to make sure you were all right. That's my job, you know."

Joshua nodded, distracted by the officer's strange comments. How had the patrolman known about the length of his trip or that he'd been helping people at the retreat? Joshua continued to consider the possibilities as he followed the officer back onto the highway and several miles south toward Phoenix. As he drove, he was pleased to realize he was no longer nodding off. The adrenaline burst, from being approached by an officer, had been enough to keep him awake for some time.

Finally the officer signaled that he was getting off at the next exit. As they approached the off-ramp, the officer exited first, taking a quick turn at the base of the hilly exit. As Joshua followed him, taking the same turn, he suddenly lost track of the motorcycle. He stopped his car and looked around. Directly ahead of him was a parking lot and a rest area complete with a gas station and all-night restaurant.

The setup was perfect. Joshua could stop for an hour or so, have some coffee and maybe a conversation with the officer, and be on his way without fear of falling asleep. He looked around, waiting for some sign of the patrolman. When he still couldn't see the officer, Joshua figured he was probably parking his motorcycle somewhere near the restaurant.

Joshua pulled into the parking lot, climbed out of his car and waited. After five minutes, he walked around the perimeter of the rest area, intent on finding the officer who had guided him to safety. Finally, he had searched every possible spot; the patrolman had vanished.

Years of work in Christian ministry, years of serving at his local church had not prepared him for the feeling that swept over him at that moment—suddenly he understood. There was only one way the officer could have known about Joshua's weekend and his bare feet.

The officer must have been an angel, sent by God to protect him from falling asleep. And Joshua was certain he would have nodded off within minutes if it hadn't been for the officer.

There was still one way to find out. Remembering clearly the officer's badge number, Joshua headed toward the all-night diner and walked up to a pay phone just outside the front door. He found the local highway patrol listed in the phone booth's Yellow Pages and dialed the number.

"I need to know the name of an officer," he told the receptionist. "He helped me out a little while ago and I want to thank him."

"Badge number?"

"Three, seven," Joshua said, remembering vividly each number as he had seen it on the officer's badge.

There was a pause. "Three, seven, is that all?"

"Yes."

"Are you sure?"

"Yes," Joshua said. "Positive."

"Well, you must be thinking of something else," she said strangely. "We don't have any officers with that badge number. Nothing even close. Our officers have numbers with three digits."

It was true, Joshua told himself as he hung up the telephone. From that moment on, Joshua believed that the officer had been an angel, sent to save him from certain death if he had fallen asleep while driving the interstate.

"Thank you, God," he said quietly, gazing toward the star-covered sky before climbing back into his car that night. "Thank you for protecting me."

Her Father's Face

JOANIE EVERETT HAD ALWAYS BEEN CLOSE TO HER FATHER. When Joanie was a little girl growing up in Pennsylvania, Larry Everett would come home from work and spend hours playing with his little girl.

In the 1940s and 1950s, the two continued to be close as Joanie reached adolescence and then adulthood. They shared a love for athletics and the outdoors and often hiked around the lake near their home. Larry was his daughter's fiercest protector and the first one with a listening ear when she was at a crossroads in life. Their home was always a place of love and family fun.

Then, when Joanie was only twenty-five years old, her father became ill with cancer. He died a few months later. The loss of the man who had been such a central part of her life was overwhelming, and for months her mother worried about whether she would ever be the same again.

Since her father's death, Joanie had dropped out of college and did little more than clean the house and stay in the tiny bedroom she had grown up in. She also lost weight, and dark circles appeared under her once-bright blue eyes.

"Joanie, you need to get out of the house, meet people," Sarah Everett would tell her daughter. "Your father would never have wanted you wasting away like this in his absence."

Joanie knew her mother was right, but there was an emptiness inside her that she could neither escape nor explain. Months passed with little change in Joanie's depression. Then sometime near the anniversary of Larry's death, Joanie and two of her friends, Jill and Pamela, decided to hike along a lake that had been one of Larry Everett's favorite spots.

"I'm not sure we should be doing this," Joanie said as she and the others got out of the car and headed toward the lake. Parts of the hike would be hilly, and Joanie didn't feel she had the energy to scale the hills, not to mention the memories she would certainly encounter.

"Come on, Joanie. It's time," Jill said. She gently pulled Joanie's arm and led the slender, brown-haired young woman toward the trail.

Joanie nodded. "I know. Now or never." She took a deep breath and headed toward the lake, following her two friends.

For nearly thirty minutes, the threesome walked in silence, each lost in her own thoughts. Joanie forced herself to continue forward as the memories of her father bombarded her with an almost physical force. The three friends turned a corner to approach the steepest hill of the climb. The path followed the hill straight up and then leveled off along a fifty-yard plateau. At the top of the hill, a bench marked the spot where Joanie and her father had often sat and talked when they visited the lake.

Joanie swallowed hard and stared straight ahead. She would have to take the hill by storm, facing every memory along the way and refusing to give in to her overwhelming feelings of grief.

Then suddenly she saw someone on the hill high above her.

A tall man in a trenchcoat was standing on the plateau staring out at the lake. From her viewpoint, the man looked exactly like her dead father. Joanie gasped, but her friends did not seem to hear her, and the trio continued up the hill. As they did, Joanie kept her eyes on the man, and suddenly, she felt a burden being lifted from her shoulders. When they were just ten yards from the man, he turned toward Joanie and smiled the same warm and reassuring smile that had once belonged to Larry Everett alone.

Joanie's friends still seemed oblivious to the man and continued past him without stopping. When Joanie was only a few feet away from him, she paused and stared into his eyes. He winked once, smiled again, and then slowly turned back toward the lake.

At that instant, Joanie had no doubt that somehow this man was her father. There was no way anyone could look so much like him and be anyone else. She seemed to know, instinctively, that there was no need to question the man or engage in dialogue. A peaceful reassurance washed over her. She continued her hike, never even looking back at the man. Later, at the bottom of the hill, she asked her friends to stop a moment.

"Did you see him?" she asked. Immediately her friends noticed a different look in Joanie's eyes. Finally, after months of grieving, she seemed at peace with herself.

"Who?" Jill asked, with a blank look.

"Yeah, who?" Pamela said.

Joanie cocked her head curiously. "That man, up on the top of the hill." She turned and pointed toward the hill, but the man had vanished. "He was up there, near the bench."

Jill and Pamela assured Joanie that they hadn't seen anyone at the top of the hill. At that moment, Joanie felt another wave of peace and again somehow knew that it was not necessary to share the experience.

"Never mind," Joanie said quickly, resuming her walk. "Must have been my imagination."

Jill and Pamela shrugged; Joanie was thankful they dropped the subject. Whoever the man was, he had given her a glimpse of the father she so badly missed and the reassurance that she had desperately needed. She would keep the incident to herself for a while and savor it. And regardless of what anyone else would say to doubt it, from that point on Joanie was convinced that an angel bearing an uncanny resemblance to her father had been and would always be watching over her.

This notion was confirmed five years later when Joanie was working in Washington, D.C., near the Smithsonian Institute. She had gone into town for lunch and was returning along Tenth Street when she paused at the curb, waiting for the light to change.

Suddenly, she felt the firm grasp of a hand on her shoulder that pulled her back, away from the curb. The force from the hand was so strong, it nearly knocked her onto the ground. At the exact same instant, a city bus traveling along Tenth Street turned right at that intersection and jumped the curb directly where Joanie had been standing. If she had remained standing there, she'd have been killed.

She turned at once to thank the person who had rescued her, but there was no one within fifty feet of her. Again she felt an overwhelming sense of peace and reassurance.

Joanie is convinced that the person who saved her life was not of this world and that had she seen him, he would have borne a strong resemblance to her dead father.

Heavenly Protection

∾

ONG BEFORE HE AND HIS WIFE, JENNY, traveled to New Hebrides Islands to spread God's word, the Reverend Stewart G. Michel felt drawn toward mission work. He had completed his education and training, and finally, in 1973, he and Jenny had boarded a series of airplanes and moved to the islands.

"Are you afraid, Stewart?" Jenny had whispered as they arrived at the thatched-roof, single-room dwelling where they were to live and work as missionaries for the next year.

Stewart smiled calmly. Jenny was more concerned than he about the obstacles they would certainly face on the islands. Disease, deadly animals, and fierce natives all figured to play a factor in their lives for the next year. But Stewart was not worried, and he gently took Jenny's hand in his.

"Sweetheart, you know we'll be fine here," he said softly. "God will protect us."

Jenny nodded, looking anxiously at their surroundings. Everything seemed so foreign, so completely different than anything she'd seen before. There were no supermarkets, no paved roads, nothing to offer the security she'd known all her life.

"You're worried, aren't you?" Stewart asked, squeezing her hand and looking into her deep blue eyes.

Jenny laughed nervously. "Is it that obvious?"

"Yes," Stewart replied, with empathy. "Listen, I understand, really. But we have prayed for God's protection, Jenny. Do you believe He hears us?"

Jenny nodded quickly. "Of course I believe."

"Well, then we have to trust. God brought us here for a reason, and He's going to see us through."

They had shared the conversation a hundred times during their preparation for this mission. But now, with their new home sitting just fifty feet away, there was something more real about the reassurance Jenny felt. She smiled and climbed out of their beat-up van, pulling Stewart along with her.

"OK, come on then," she had said, the hesitation gone from her voice. "We have a mission to run!"

That had been six months earlier. They had learned to deal with the disease, equipped as they were with various medicines and vaccines. And they had developed ways to stay clear from the wild animals that lived in the brush near their home. Best of all, they were finding ample opportunities to hold Bible studies throughout the area and to teach the local tribes about their faith. But there was one tribe—known for its fierce fighting techniques—which grew more hostile toward them with each passing day. For weeks they had threatened to attack the Michels and kill them because they had interfered with ancient tribal traditions and taught their people a new and strange way of thinking.

Finally, the hostile tribe made plans to carry out their threats. Late in the evening of June 23, the Michels lay in their small bed and listened to the sound of war cries growing louder and louder.

"They're coming for us, Stewart," a terrified Jenny whispered in the dark of their bungalow.

Stewart nodded. "Keep praying, Jenny. Keep praying."

Jenny squeezed her eyes tight, trying to force the frightening sounds from her mind. But they grew still closer until their shrill screams and chanting surrounded the Michels's dwelling.

Stewart began to pray aloud.

"Heavenly Father," he began, "you have told us to ask for anything in your means. We come before you now and ask you to protect us as you have in the past. Please deliver us from the danger we are in."

For nearly an hour the sounds continued outside the bungalow. At the end of the hour, the Michels could see dancing lights surrounding their home.

"Fire," Stewart whispered, holding Jenny tightly. "Keep praying. I think they might try to burn us out."

Jenny gasped and buried her face in Stewart's shoulder.

Another fifteen minutes passed while the Michels continued to pray for protection. Then, suddenly, the screaming began to lessen and grow gradually more distant. "They're leaving!" Jenny said, and her muscles began to relax.

The couple lay listening in the darkness as the tribesmen moved farther and farther away. Finally their menacing sounds disappeared altogether.

"Thank you, Father," Stewart said aloud, gazing toward the sky. "Thank you for protecting us. Thank you for delivering us."

Three months went by, and the Michels had no explanation for why the tribesmen chose not to kill them that terrifying night. Then, in a strange turn of events, the chief of that tribe contacted the Michels and began asking questions about their mission work and about Jesus Christ. Before the end of the year, the chief converted to Christianity. At that time Stewart Michel decided to ask the question that had burned in his mind for nearly a year.

"Why didn't you kill us that night?" he asked, staring gently into the chief's eyes.

The chief nodded. "We tried," he said. "But your guards wouldn't let us past."

Stewart's eyes narrowed in confusion. "What guards?"

The chief waved his arms dramatically. "Hundreds of guards, big men in shining clothes with swords drawn and torches," he said excitedly in broken English. But the missionary understood every word.

"Where did they come from?" he asked, baffled at the chief's story about what had taken place that awful night.

"Your guards," the chief repeated, as if the Michels should know where their protection came from. "Circled your hut, hundreds of them. Big men. Never seen anything like that before. We had no choice. We left."

Suddenly Michel thought he understood. Chills ran along his neck and down his arms. Hadn't they prayed for protection? Didn't God use angels as a way of taking care of his people? When Michel shared the story with Jenny, she agreed with him.

"God's protection came in the form of a hundred angels dressed like guards and stationed around our home," Jenny says when she talks of the event. "Who else could they have been but angels?"

Point the Way

ℭ

HEN WILLIAM LANDEMANN SET OUT FOR A HIKE around one of the frozen lakes near the University of Wisconsin at Madison, he knew nothing of the impending blizzard headed in his direction. At twenty-one years old, Landemann was an advanced hiker and backpacker with years of experience in the Great Lakes area hunting, fishing, and wandering the woods. He shared an off-campus apartment with two friends, and although he spent much of his time at school, he still preferred the solitude of the outdoors. It was only while outdoors, amidst undisturbed nature, that William felt truly connected with God.

Landemann had been raised a traditional Catholic but found the church to be too confining. He believed that God was bigger than weekly rituals and lists of rules, and when he was alone amidst nature he would spend hours praying and growing close to his Creator.

That cold February morning in 1975 was no different than many others like it. Landemann was in the habit of leaving the house without word to his roommates. He would spend most of the day alone in the wilderness that surrounded the edge of the university. He wore a down parka, boots, mittens, and a hat, planning his trip as he set out into the sub-zero morning. The lake was about a mile from the apartment. It was a beautiful lake, twenty-five miles in circumference, nine miles long, and about five miles wide. Landemann reached its frozen edge and decided to hike onto the lake. The water had been frozen for two months, and Landemann knew the ice would be quite thick. He guessed it would take about four hours to reach the middle of the lake and return back to shore.

When he had located a point quite a distance out which he deemed to be the lake's center, he began walking. As he trudged toward the middle of the lake, Landemann noticed people skiing, playing, and fishing through ice holes in the distance. He set his mind to prayerful thoughts and the effort needed to hike through the dense snow-covered ice pack. Landemann hadn't brought water that day, so about one hour into his walk he began to eat snow to quench his thirst.

Landemann was enjoying the hike immensely, taking in the beauty around him and feeling at peace with God and himself. As he reached the midway point and started to turn back toward shore, the sky began to cloud over. Landemann thought little of the cloud cover because it was so typical of the sky in Wisconsin during the winter. Many times the clouds would gather and then by morning disappear without any storm at all. Still, he picked up his pace, certain that if a storm was headed his way he would not want to be caught in it.

Minutes later, Landemann stopped for a moment and surveyed the encroaching weather formation. He was stunned by the change in the sky. Within minutes the clouds had grown dark and dangerously low, settling almost on top of the lake's frozen surface. Landemann could feel the temperature dropping, and as he picked up his pace, once again large snowflakes began filling the air. All at once, a fierce wind swept over the lake, swirling the snowflakes, and Landemann suddenly had trouble seeing the shore. Moving as quickly as he could against the wind, Landemann estimated a ninety-minute walk before reaching the shore. With the wind against him, the hike might take as much as two hours. He forced himself to move faster.

The wind continued to increase, and in only a few minutes, Landemann could barely see his hands in front of his face. The temperature had plummeted nearly thirty degrees because of the sudden storm. Landemann leaned heavily into the wind and continued to walk, losing track of time and pulling his arms close to his body in an effort to fight the effects of hypothermia. The blizzard grew even more fierce, and suddenly, Landemann stumbled onto the ice. When he opened his eyes, he realized he could see nothing but white. Even his hands had disappeared from sight. He fell in a heap, unable to move because of his sudden dizziness and inability to distinguish up from down. He was disoriented and could not move without falling. Then Landemann realized what had happened. He was snow-blind.

In the years since he had first begun backpacking and exploring the forests near his home, Landemann had read about people who had been trapped in sudden blizzards and become snow-blind. The condition was a deadly one, because once it happened, a person could become completely disoriented and freeze to death, sometimes only inches from safety.

Landemann pushed the thoughts from his mind and forced himself into a prone position on the ice.

"I've got to keep moving," he ordered himself aloud. "Keep moving!"

Reaching forward he dug his fingers into the snow and pulled his body forward. Now and then he would hear deep, powerful groans from beneath the lake's frozen surface.

"Help me!" he shouted, suddenly concerned that the ice would crack and he would drown in the freezing water. But his cries for help were swallowed up immediately by the force of the wind. At least he could move.

Time passed and Landemann was struck by another frightening thought. What if he had been crawling in circles, wasting valuable energy and getting no closer to the shore? He stopped and dropped his head onto the snow and ice, closing his eyes to shut out the horrifying blinding white that consumed him.

"Please, dear God, help me find my way!" he shouted. Tears filled his eyes and froze on his cheeks as he realized the gravity of his situation.

At that moment, Landemann heard the deep resonant sound of the foghorn which was located at the rescue station at the edge of the lake, just blocks from his house. For the first time in nearly thirty minutes Landemann had a reference point, a way to determine which way he was headed. Then he heard the sound of a voice speaking over the rescue station's private address system. "Be careful," the voice said clearly and loudly. "The breakwater is open and deep."

Landemann understood. He must have wandered close to the breakwater, where the ice was broken and the water treacherously deep. He began slithering toward the voice. Again he heard a warning. "Be careful, stay to the right, climb the concrete wall when you reach it."

The voice pushed Landemann forward and filled him with hope. He knew if he could continue toward the voice and ultimately the rescue station, he would find safety. Soon he could hear the waves near the breakwater, and he obeyed the voice, staying to the right. Because he had used his hands to pull himself forward, he had lost nearly all feeling in them. But somehow, he reached the wall, still on his belly. He looked up, his body aching from exertion and the beginnings of hypothermia, and he saw the light from the rescue station ahead. He climbed over the retaining wall and felt his way through deep drifts of snow to the door of the rescue station.

A moment later the door opened, and he could feel himself being pulled inside by a large man. When Landemann had caught his breath and could open his eyes, the bearded man helped him into a chair and offered him a mug of hot coffee.

"Thank you," Landemann said, too stunned to say anything else, though his heart was full. Instead, Landemann stared at the man who had saved his life and was intrigued by his strangely peaceful nature.

The man moved to a table across the room and smiled at Landemann. "You were lost out there," he said softly, standing to refill Landemann's cup.

Landemann nodded. "Yes, I didn't know where I was. Couldn't see anything."

The man stared directly at Landemann. His eyes were crystal blue, a color Landemann had never seen before.

"Yes, I know. I knew you were lost so I sounded the foghorn. Then I sent out some advice about the breakwater, in case you had lost your bearings."

"Good timing," Landemann said, baffled at the way in which God had used this man to help him to safety.

As they spoke, Landemann realized that the weather had cleared up.

"Thank you again. I best be heading back," he told the man, who continued to sit at the table without any apparent task at hand. Suddenly Landemann was curious. "Why were you here, anyway?" he asked. Normally the lake's rescue station is closed down for winter.

"Doing research," the man said, smiling gently.

Landemann nodded, satisfied with the answer. He thanked the man again, the two said their goodbyes, and Landemann walked home. Not until he was safely inside his apartment did Landemann realize he had been gone for seven hours. He told his roommates about his experience.

"That's impossible," said Dana, one of Landemann's roommates. "The station closes down in the winter," she said absently. "Must have been some other building or something."

"No, it was the rescue station," Landemann said adamantly. "I know it's usually closed down by now, but this guy there really helped me. Said he was doing research or something."

His roommates looked at him doubtfully.

"The place has been closed down," Dana said once again. "I went by there the other day. Closed for winter."

"Listen, guys, I'm not losing my mind! I can still taste the coffee. Hey, he saved my life. He was there, and a good thing, too."

"I guess," Dana admitted. The roommates agreed that whoever the man had been, Landemann was certainly lucky he had been at the rescue station and seen him at just the right time.

After a long night's sleep, Landemann awoke the next morning determined to find the man and thank him again for saving his life. He dressed warmly and walked to the rescue building. As he approached, he suddenly grew confused. The station was locked tightly, its concrete-bunker design lifeless and imposing. Puzzled, Landemann made his way to the front door, but found it nearly buried under a snow drift, which showed no signs of having been disturbed in weeks, if not months.

There had been no snow since the sudden storm the day before. The snow in front of the door should have been cleared away or, at least, there should have been obvious signs of tracks leading up and down the steps. Feeling more than a bit odd, Landemann dug through the drift to the door and found a sign which read: "Closed for winter (October 1975 to April 1976)."

But if the rescue station had been closed, locked with chains from the outside and partially buried under snow drifts, how had the man gotten inside? Furthermore, how had *he* gotten inside in the minutes after finding his way off the lake and out of the blizzard? Landemann stood motionless, going over the details of the day before in his mind. He knew this was the place he had come to. This was where the man had poured him hot coffee and helped him off the lake. The only foghorn in the area was located here at the rescue station.

Suddenly, Landemann knew there was one other way to check on the man's identity. He hurried home to call the county sheriff's department, which had jurisdiction over the building.

"No one has had access to the rescue station since it was closed down in the fall, Mr Landemann," he was told. Landemann continued to search for information, dialing the local university to see if anyone had been given permission to do research at the building.

"No, the county doesn't allow any research at the rescue station during the off-season."

Landemann hung up the phone and fell to his knees, weak with the realization. Then he remembered his prayer and the way he had felt so close to God moments before the storm appeared.

"Could it have been?" he whispered to himself. "Is it possible?"

Although there would never be any way to prove what had happened that stormy afternoon, Landemann had made his mind up. From that point on, Landemann believed he had been helped by an angel who chose to save his life in what was a very special encounter.

Angel in a Yellow
Snow-Removal Vehicle

❧

I N THE WINTER OF 1972, life was exactly what Dennis O'Neill wanted it to be. He had been preparing for the priesthood since graduating from high school, eleven years ago, and now he was just one year from his ordination. That winter, he was serving as a deacon for a parish in one of the northwest suburbs of Chicago, Illinois. His work kept him in constant contact with the parishioners, and he was developing a gift for helping people grow closer to God. He knew he had done the right thing by pursuing a life in the priesthood.

One evening, just before midnight, Dennis was driving southeast into Chicago during a blinding blizzard. As he reached the intersection of the Kennedy and Edens expressways—a crossing where more than eight lanes of traffic come together—his car hit a patch of black ice and began to spin out of control.

Dennis bore down hard on the brakes but his car only spun faster, moving directly into heavy oncoming traffic. Although his car continued to spin violently, Dennis managed to catch sight of a Volkswagon which was about to slam into his car. The other vehicle was so close, Dennis could clearly see its driver, even in the blowing snow. Dennis closed his eyes, bracing himself for what would certainly be a violent and painful impact.

"This is it!" he thought to himself.

But nothing happened. He opened his eyes slowly and found that his car had inexplicably stopped spinning. Directly in front of him was a large yellow snow-removal vehicle. The enormous truck-sized snow scraper had somehow protected Dennis from being hit by the Volkswagon or any other car. The driver, a middle-aged man with warm brown eyes and a baseball cap, motioned to Dennis that everything was all right and that he would shield Denniss's car until he was ready to resume driving.

Somehow, at the same time that he was stopped short and amidst utter confusion, Dennis experienced an unnatural silence. Even the traffic racing by on either side of him seemed to be making no noise. Dennis inched forward, turning his car in the right direction. Before driving away, he glanced in his rearview mirror and saw the driver of the snow-removal vehicle wave reassuringly. Dennis waved back and then drove away.

Moments later, his body began to shudder uncontrollably as he realized how close he had come to being involved in a severe car accident. The more he thought about the incident, the harder he began to shake, unable to understand what had happened. Where had the yellow vehicle come from? How had the cumbersome snowplow gotten between him and the oncoming cars? Why hadn't any of the cars crashed into him before the driver of the snowplow could position his vehicle safely in front of Denniss's?

Finally, as his body began to relax, Dennis realized there was only one answer. The hand of God had shielded him from certain death. With this realization, a feeling of peace washed over him.

Seven years passed and Dennis—by that time Father O'Neill—never forgot how God had helped him that cold winter night.

One day while serving as a priest at Saint Thomas the Apostle Church in Chicago, Father O'Neill asked a class of eighth-graders to share their personal experiences of how God had worked in their lives. As an example, he shared his story about the snow-removal vehicle.

"Ever since that winter of 1972, a snow-removal vehicle has been for me a symbol of God's love and protection," he told the wide-eyed group.

The next day, on an unusually warm and balmy May afternoon, Father O'Neill was driving a friend home from downtown Chicago when suddenly his right front tire experienced a blowout. Although it was the only blowout Father O'Neill had ever had, he knew how to change a tire; he carefully pulled his car off to the side of the road. As his car came to a stop, he glanced in the rearview mirror before opening the door.

There, pulling off the road behind him, was a large yellow snow-removal vehicle. Father O'Neill's eyes opened wide in surprise. He could not remember seeing any such vehicle on the expressway; there hadn't been an on-ramp for more than a mile. Father O'Neill remained in his car, watching the snow-removal vehicle and its driver, unable to imagine where either one had come from.

Slowly, the driver climbed out and walked up to Father O'Neill. He had warm, kind brown eyes and wore a baseball cap. He was smiling calmly. Before hearing him speak, Father O'Neill felt a silent reassurance coming from the man.

"Everything OK?" he asked.

"Yes, thanks," Father O'Neill said quickly. "Tire blew but I can change it."

"OK then, I'll be on my way," the man said, nodding his head and tipping the baseball cap. "I just wanted to make sure."

With that, the man turned around and climbed back into the snow-removal vehicle. As he drove away, he waved once more to the awe-struck priest.

To this day, Father O'Neill does not know exactly who the driver of the yellow snow-removal vehicle was or how such a large winter vehicle suddenly appeared on the Dan Ryan Expressway in late May. But he is as certain now as he was then that God is watching over him wherever he goes, using a number of means to assure his protection. Even, quite possibly, an angel at the wheel of a large, yellow snow-removal vehicle.

Christmas Angel of Hope

∽

HE STORY OF HOPE was an integral part of Phyllis Scott's Christmas memories, and she would forever be touched when she shared it.

Back in 1911, when she was four and her brother, two, their parents, Jack and Martha, often struggled financially. Still, they shared an especially close bond, and there was always enough food and love to go around.

That Christmas week was a troublesome one for the Scott family because Phyllis's little brother, Tommy, was sick; he had a high temperature, and the doctors feared he might have polio. In those days, there were no vaccines for polio, and many children died from that disease. Throughout the days and nights that preceded Christmas, Jack and. Martha took turns kneeling by their sick little boy's bed and praying for his recovery.

In addition to the child's illness, there were other troubles that Christmas. The mill where Jack worked had cut his hours in recent weeks, and they had been unable to afford Christmas presents for the children. Martha had been secretly knitting socks and scarves, but her dream of buying Phyllis and Tommy a toy each and some candy had been shattered. Now it was all they could do to purchase food and other necessities.

The Scotts spent Christmas Eve gathered in Tommy's bedroom praying and singing carols and sponging the boy's feverish body. After a long and restless night, the Scotts finally fell exhausted into their own beds.

Very early on Christmas morning, when Martha was up fixing breakfast and arranging the wrapped parcels of socks and scarves by the children's plates, she heard a loud knocking sound. Martha tilted her head curiously and wiped her hands on her apron as she moved toward the front door.

"Yes," she said as she opened it.

There, on the front porch, was a handsome, well-dressed man and a pretty little girl. A large white dog stood at the child's side.

"Merry Christmas, Mrs Scott," the stranger said in a soft voice filled with kindness. "I've come to see how Tommy is doing."

Martha stood staring at the man and child on her porch, unable to comprehend how a stranger might know her name and the name of her child.

"Do I know you?"

The man ignored the question. "How is the child, Mrs Scott?"

"Sir, who are you?" she asked. There was an unusual presence about the man and she was not afraid, but she wanted very much to know the identity of the stranger before her.

The man shook his head politely and smiled. "I came only to find out the condition of your son, ma'am," he said.

Still flustered, Martha ran her hand through her hair and took a deep breath and decided to answer the man. "Well, he's only a little boy, two years old," she began.

The man nodded kindly and the little girl beside him smiled. Martha continued.

"He's always been in good health until about a week ago when he caught this fever and—" she paused and her voice cracked. "Doctor says it might be polio."

"I know," the man said softly, reaching out toward Martha and squeezing her hand. "But he will recover shortly."

Tears began streaming down Martha's face, which she wiped away quickly.

"Please, sir," she said, her face contorted in confusion. "Come in out of the cold and tell me who you are, how you know our names."

Again the man smiled and shook his head. "We must be going now," he said. "Close the door quickly so the cold doesn't get to the boy's room."

"But wait…"

The man waved once. Then he and the child and the big, white dog turned around and walked down the porch steps. Although he had cautioned her to close the door, Martha stood on the porch watching the trio to see where they were headed. Just as they reached the last step, Jack called out from the back room and Martha turned away. When she looked toward the porch again, the man, the little girl, and the dog had disappeared.

Martha ran quickly down the porch steps and scanned the street in both directions, but the sidewalks were empty. Dazed by what had happened, she walked slowly back into the house and shared the story with her husband.

"Who could he have possibly been?" she asked him.

"I don't know, Martha," Jack said. Then he smiled. "Maybe he was sent by God. A Christmas present to assure us that little Tommy is going to be all right."

The couple pondered this and before waking the children, they prayed again for their sick son.

"I'm going to check on Tommy," Martha said as she stood up from the table. "You get Phyllis and tell her to come downstairs for Christmas breakfast."

A few minutes later, when Jack was in Phyllis's room waking the girl and wishing her a Merry Christmas, he heard Martha.

"Jack, come quickly," she shouted.

Jack grabbed Phyllis's hand and the two ran down the hallway toward Tommy's room.

"What is it?" Jack was frightened; perhaps Tommy had grown worse or he might not have survived the night.

When they entered the little boy's room, Jack saw Martha sitting on the bed, her eyes glistening with unshed tears as Tommy sat grinning in her arms. She reached for her husband's hand.

"Jack, the fever's gone. He seems completely better," she whispered.

"Dear God," Jack whispered, and slowly, he knelt on the floor beside the child's bed. The Scott family held hands and thanked God for healing Tommy.

"And thank you, too, God, for the stranger this morning. Thank you for giving us hope."

They did not see or hear from the strange man again until three years later, in April 1914. This time he was alone, but when Martha answered the door, she knew instantly that this was the same man who had visited them that Christmas morning.

"You've come again!" Martha said, opening the door and waving an arm toward her living room. "Please come in. I want to know your name, who you are."

But just as before, the man smiled and shook his head. "I wanted to tell you I'm sorry about your husband losing his job. But he will be working again soon."

This time before Martha could say another word, the man smiled warmly, tipped his hat politely, and turned quickly to leave. Martha called after him and watched as he turned around the corner of the house and headed toward the thick woods in back of their home. Martha ran down the steps after him, but by the time she got to the back of the house, there was no one in sight and not a sound from anywhere. Again, the man had disappeared.

Shocked by his visitation, Martha returned to the house and convinced herself that she must have been imagining things. The man must have been a different person, and he must have had the wrong house. After all, Jack had not lost his job. She silently thanked God that her husband did, in fact, have a job, and tried to forget about the stranger at the door.

That night, Jack came home from work earlier than usual with his shoulders slumped in defeat. He pulled Martha slowly into a tight hug and then sat her down gently on their worn sofa.

"I have some bad news," he said, looking deeply into her eyes. "I was laid off today."

Martha felt her heart skip a beat at her husband's words. The stranger had been right after all. She sighed deeply and told Jack about the visit from the stranger earlier that day.

"He said you'd be back working again soon," she said as she finished the story. "Jack, who is he?"

Jack shook his head in awe. "Whoever he is, he seems to want to bring us hope. Remember that Christmas morning when we wondered if Tommy was going to make it? He already knew everything was going to be all right and wanted to give us the same peace of mind. Maybe it's true. Maybe we have nothing to worry about now, either."

Martha nodded. "Well, let's go eat dinner. At least for now we still have food on the table." She moved to take off her apron, then suddenly she gasped.

"Jack!" she screamed. "Look!"

In her hand, she held a twenty-dollar bill, which had been nestled in her apron pocket. "Twenty dollars, Jack! Where in the world did it come from?"

For a moment Jack and Martha were silent, and then, at the same time, both reached the same conclusion.

"The stranger?" Martha asked quietly. Jack nodded and took her hand.

"Maybe he was more than a stranger, Martha. Maybe he was our guardian angel. It's possible, isn't it?"

For days, the couple pondered the stranger and his message. Then, two weeks later, Jack's job was restored, and he was given a bonus check for returning to the position. After that, the Scotts were convinced that whoever the man was, he was neither human nor ordinary. He had known their names and their needs, and he had brought them hope in times of despair.

Each year until Martha died, her faith remained strong as she told the story of the stranger who came bearing hope. The Christmas angel, she liked to call him.

In many ways, the stranger is still spreading hope today, as the story, which now belongs to Phyllis, continues to be passed down among the children, grandchildren, and great-grandchildren of Jack and Martha Scott.

Divine Direction

 R. CHARLES MADISON HAD ALWAYS WONDERED what his life might have been like if he had been a missionary. His parents had known several missionaries, and as a boy, Charles would listen to their stories, dreaming of someday traveling to far-off countries, where he could tell people about the love of Jesus.

Instead, he worked his way through medical school and became an emergency room doctor, working at a hospital near his home, in Glendora. He never regretted his decision to work in the medical field, viewing it as a form of missionary work, in that he worked daily with people and had been given numerous opportunities to share his faith in the process. Regardless of his hectic schedule, Dr. Madison always remained an active member of his local church, and by the early 1980s, he had developed friendships with several missionaries.

When he was able to take some vacation time in 1981, Dr. Madison arranged a vacation to Bangalore, India, where he planned to visit his missionary friends and experience their lifestyle.

"I'm just a little unsure about how to make the transfer when I stop in Bombay," Dr. Madison admitted to his friends in a final telephone call before making the trip. His air transportation took him through the Bombay Airport, where he would have to catch a connecting flight to Bangalore.

"Don't worry," his friends told him. "God will get you here."

When Dr. Madison boarded the plane in Los Angeles headed for Bombay, he recalled those words and wondered how the transfer would work out. He relaxed and didn't think about the situation again until the plane landed many hours later. He stood up and stretched, grabbed his carry-on bag, and made his way down a flight of stairs toward the main building.

Dr. Madison checked his watch as he entered the airport, which even at 4 a.m. was teeming with people. He had less than thirty minutes to catch his connecting flight to Bangalore. Walking to the first airline counter he could see, Dr. Madison smiled and began to speak.

"I'm looking for Flight 457, connecting from Bombay to Bangalore," he said slowly.

But the man shook his head quickly. "No," he fairly shouted. "No, no. No English!"

Dr. Madison understood by the man's gestures that he did not speak English. Glancing about the airport, Dr. Madison realized that although many people in Bombay speak fluent English, he could see no signs in English. He asked several more airline representatives, but after fifteen minutes, he still had no idea about which direction to go to catch his flight. He found his luggage but no one who could point him in the right direction.

Just when Dr. Madison began to wonder where he would go if he missed his plane, a man walked up to him dressed in standard American business clothing.

"Come this way," the man said in a voice that was authoritative but kind. The man turned his back on Dr. Madison and began walking.

"Hey, you don't know where I need to go," he yelled at the man, who was rapidly walking away. When the man did not respond, Dr. Madison shrugged and realized that he had no other options. He picked up his suitcase and followed the man. They walked the length of the airport, and the doctor followed the man outside where a bus was waiting at the curb.

"Get on here," the man said in the same commanding voice. When Dr.

Madison climbed onto the bus, the man followed and took a seat opposite him.

"So, where are we going?" the doctor asked curiously.

"You need to catch a flight to Bangalore, correct?" the man asked in response.

Dr. Madison nodded, wondering how the man might have had that information.

"The domestic flights leave from the airport down the highway. The bus will take us there."

Dr. Madison nodded. "Where are you from?"

The man paused a moment. "I'm just home on break," he said.

Just then, the bus pulled up in front of the domestic airport.

"Hey, thanks a lot," Dr. Madison said appreciatively. "I would never have known about this place. No one around there spoke English."

"Yes," the man answered, glancing out the window. "I know. You'll be fine now."

Dr. Madison walked toward the door of the bus and stepped out, reaching up into the bus's luggage rack located on the outside of the bus next to the passenger door. He waited a moment for the man to follow him, but when no one came out, Dr. Madison stepped back inside the bus.

The man was gone.

Dr. Madison moved backward and stood beside the bus completely stunned. The man definitely had not left the bus; Dr. Madison had been standing beside the exit and would have seen him. But where had he gone? And how had he known exactly where he needed to go to catch his flight? Another thing bothered Dr. Madison. If he was an American, how could he be home on break in India? The doctor stepped inside the bus once more and looked carefully around, making certain the man was not still inside. Finally he shook his head, picked up his suitcase and caught his connecting flight to Bangalore.

Once he had arrived and was seated around the kitchen table with his missionary friends, he shared his story.

"Maybe he was an angel, Charles," one of his friends said, his voice serious.

Dr. Madison was quiet for a moment. "I never thought about it. But I guess it's possible."

"Of course it's possible. God works in strange ways sometimes."

After that, Dr. Madison put the incident behind him. He was never sure whether the man had actually been an angel, but at the same time he had no other explanation for his assistance and then disappearance. In the years that followed, Dr. Madison's practice grew busy, as did his personal life. He got married and was very satisfied with the direction his life was taking. He did not think about the incident in Bombay until about four years later when he decided to visit the same missionary friends, who by then were in Kenya.

This time his travels took him through the Pakistan airport. He got off the plane and was instantly in the familiar situation of looking for an English-speaking person to guide him toward the right terminal. None of the signs were in English, and Charles suddenly remembered his experience in Bombay as if it were only a day or so ago. He set his suitcase down and looked around, desperately searching for someone to give him directions.

Suddenly, a man dressed in traditional Indian garb approached him.

"You need to go this way," the man said, speaking in perfect English. He pointed toward a nearby terminal where travelers were lining up and about to board an airplane. Dr. Madison picked up his luggage and turned to thank the man. As in Bombay, the man was suddenly gone. Dr. Madison stood stuck in place, chills running down his spine. The man could not have gotten away so quickly.

Later that evening, when the doctor arrived in Kenya, he wasted no time in sharing the event with his friends, this time suggesting to them that the man had indeed been an angel.

"Remember the man who helped me in Bombay?" Dr. Madison asked.

"Sure, he steered you in the right direction and then disappeared, right?"

Dr. Madison nodded. "Well, you were right about him, because it happened again."

"You mean about him being an angel?"

"I have no doubt. God is really something, isn't he? Helping me out like that when I felt completely lost."

"Nothing new about that, my friend," one of the missionaries said, a smile covering his face. "If only we will listen, God will always point us in the right direction."

Dr. Madison was silent a moment, thinking of how he had felt guided into a medical career and of the other events in his life. He had grown up believing God was always watching over him. But now he had a different, more real understanding of that truth. "You know," he said, his eyes warm with the knowledge of God's very real presence, "I think you're right."

Miracle in the Mundane

HAT WARM JUNE IN 1993 HAD BEEN HECTIC, and it seemed that Caryn Lessur had been late for nearly every appointment she'd made that week. Her husband, Donny, a high school teacher, was in his last week of instruction at the private school where he taught in West Hills. It was 2:10 in the afternoon and Caryn knew she had to pick her husband up at school by 2:30.

"I only need a few things," she told herself aloud as she pulled into the parking lot of the grocery store, across the street from the school. Gently lifting her four-month-old son and grabbing her wallet, she dashed into the store. Once inside, however, she found several additional items the family needed and quickly filled a cart with groceries.

With the baby's carrier in one cart, she needed two carts to get all the bags out to the car. A market clerk offered to push one of them.

With only two minutes before she was to meet Donny, she hurried to open the car's trunk, directing the clerk to place the bags inside.

"Thanks for the help," Caryn said, smiling as she took her tiny son from the other cart and strapped him in his seat inside the car. As she was doing so, the clerk took both carts and began pushing them back toward the store.

"I'll take care of the carts," she yelled toward Caryn, who was still getting her son situated. "Have a good day."

"Thanks," Caryn said, and then slipped into the front seat. At that moment she realized that she had left her wallet on the top seat of one of the shopping carts. She turned around and saw that the clerk had gone inside. There was no telling where the cart was.

Glancing at her watch, Caryn took her son out of the car once again and ran back into the store toward the clerk.

"My wallet, did you see it?" she asked, out of breath and nervous.

A blank look fell upon the clerk's face. "Wallet?"

Caryn nodded frantically. "It was on the top seat of the cart. Where'd you take them?"

The clerk pointed outside. "Out there with the others."

"OK. Thanks."

Caryn rushed outside, still holding her baby, and looked at the long row of carts. She quickly guessed that there might be as many as a hundred carts lined up in front of the store. Still, the cart would have to be near the front or back of the line because only a few minutes had passed. She raced toward the front of the line of carts and began looking inside each one. The wallet was not to be found.

Frustrated and aware that she was already ten minutes late for Donny, Caryn went back inside the store and asked about the wallet at the store's lost-and-found section.

"Nothing's been turned in, ma'am," the girl said. "Can I get your name and number? We'll call you if we find anything."

Caryn nodded quickly and jotted down the information. Then she began racing through the store asking each shopper if they had taken a cart from outside and if they had found a wallet in it. But each time she asked the question she met with the same blank expression. No one had seen her wallet.

Finally, Caryn and her son returned to their car. As she drove across the street toward the school, Caryn made a mental checklist of everything the wallet contained: her driver's license, credit cards, her children's medical cards, numerous receipts, her automatic banking card, personal mementoes, and a book of checks. But most important of all, it contained a special picture of her and Donny taken when they were dating. Caryn began to pray.

"Lord, if there's any way, please let someone kind find my wallet so I can get it back," she prayed. "And help me to slow down."

Twenty minutes late, Caryn pulled up in front of the school and explained the entire story to her husband. The couple had been faithful Christians for six years, and Caryn wasn't surprised by her husband's words.

"I'll pray about it, too, honey," he said. "Everything will work out just fine."

"How can it?" Caryn cried. "That wallet is old, and my favorite picture of us is inside. It means so much to me, and I know I'll never see it again."

"Come on, honey. Have faith!"

Over the years, whenever Donny had reason to use those words, Caryn had been amazed at the ways God had worked out their problems. He had always provided for them, but still, at times like this, she would sometimes doubt that God could truly help.

"I feel funny asking God to help me find my wallet," Caryn admitted. "These things happen. And anyway, it was my mistake. Maybe He's trying to teach me a lesson. Telling me to slow down."

Donny shrugged and pulled her close. "Could be," he said. "Either way, things will work out. Stop worrying."

That night Caryn made several telephone calls to cancel her credit cards. But she knew there was a greater danger someone would use the driver's license and checkbook. The phone call to the bank would have to wait until business hours the next day. And she was miserable over her lost photo.

Early in the morning, Caryn called the market and asked if anyone had turned in a wallet. They hadn't, so next she called the bank and was told to come in as soon as she could. The checking account would have to be closed and a new one opened.

"You'll have to fill out several forms, then we'll close your old account. We'll make a note that the wallet was stolen, in case there are any checks written by someone other than you or your husband. Then you can open a new account and transfer the old balance," a bank teller explained over the telephone.

Caryn called Maria, a church friend who sometimes babysat for her children, and asked her to come over to babysit for an hour. When she arrived, Caryn picked up her keys and headed for the door. "Pray for me, Maria. I'm still hoping that somehow the wallet will turn up."

Caryn drove to the bank's branch where she had originally opened the bank account, even though that location was farther away than others. She sat with a bank officer for twenty minutes filling out forms. Then she was directed to wait in line for the next available teller, who would arrange a cash advance until her money could be transferred from the old account to the new.

Caryn thanked the woman and moved into line. When it was her turn, she walked up to the next available teller. As she began to explain the situation, the woman held up an object and Caryn gasped.

It was her wallet.

"How did you get it?" Caryn asked, confused and elated at the same time.

"Happened a few minutes ago," she explained. "Two young men walked in, came up to my window, and handed me the wallet. I asked them their names, but they didn't want to give them to me."

Caryn's mind raced in search of an explanation. The bank had not been busy that morning, and she had watched the customers come and go. She hadn't seen any young men in the building. Also, she had lost the wallet at a market at least seven miles away, completely across town.

Caryn took the wallet and examined it carefully. Everything was intact; not even a single credit card or receipt was missing. And the treasured photo was just where she kept it tucked, Donny's face smiling at her as they watched the sunset over Lake Tahoe that summer so many years earlier.

As she drove home, Caryn thought about Donny's faith and the way he and she had prayed about the situation. Then she thought about what had happened. The wallet had been taken by someone almost immediately after she'd lost sight of it. Caryn had spoken with every shopper at the market and looked through every cart, and since no one ever turned the wallet in at the store's lost-and-found area, the person who originally took the wallet was obviously dishonest. How, then, Caryn wondered, did the wallet wind up in the hands of the two men who returned it to the bank? And how had they known which branch to take it to? Furthermore, how was it that at the exact time Caryn was in the bank, the men had returned the wallet and handed it to the specific teller who would later wait on her?

Later when she shared the story with Donny, his eyes lit up in a knowing way. "Prayer, sweetheart."

"What about those guys?" she asked, puzzled but convinced, just as her husband was, that finding the wallet was an answer to prayer. "I know no one walked in with my wallet while I was there."

"Remember what the Bible says about angels?" Donny asked, raising one eye.

Caryn paused a moment, allowing his words to sink in. "Is it possible?" she asked, her voice filled with awe.

"What do you think?"

Neither Caryn nor Donny would ever know for sure how Caryn's wallet was returned in such an unlikely set of circumstances. And they would never know the identity of the two men who performed perhaps an angelic service amid the mundane routine of everyday life.

Unseen Angels

HE FOLLOWING STORY WAS TOLD at Lake Avenue Congregational Church in Pasadena, California, in conversation during a Sunday school class. As with several other tales told here, the names and certain details have been changed to protect the identity of the people involved. But there is something different about this story. Whereas other angel encounters in this collection involve interaction with people who quite possibly were angels, this story does not. Still, it is my opinion that an angel encounter of some kind took place, and I wanted to share it with you.

Christine Hallberg had finished shopping and was discouraged to see what time it was. The southern California mall had announced its closing message and now it was after nine o'clock. Christmas was still less than a month away, and Christine had hoped to get a great deal of shopping done before the rush began in earnest.

She gathered her bags in her arms and dug through her purse for her car keys. She knew she needed to hurry. Her husband, Mike, was home with the boys and would have been expecting her by now. Walking outside the mall into the dark, cold parking lot, Christine continued to fumble through the belongings on the bottom of her purse in search of her car keys.

Lost in her search, she did not notice the movement of at least one person very near her car.

Finally her fingers wrapped around her keys and she looked up for her car; the parking lot was nearly empty. She realized in dismay how far away she had parked. Glancing around nervously, she picked up her pace. Ten years ago she might not have worried about her safety in such a situation. But now, in 1991, crime had increased in all parts of Pasadena and the surrounding areas. Christine knew she was in a vulnerable position as she made her way to her Buick, opened the door, and climbed inside.

Suddenly, a masked man appeared less than ten feet from her window. His eyes were wild and he was walking toward her, pointing a gun at her, and motioning for her to open the door.

Resisting the urge to panic, Christine ignored the man, locked her door, and tried to start her car. Nothing happened. The man was nearly at her door; she tried again, but the engine seemed to be completely dead.

"Please, God!" she whispered, just as the man began banging the handle of the gun on her window.

Closing her eyes, Christine tried once more to start the car, and finally, the engine turned over. In an instant, Christine slammed the car into gear and sped off, leaving the man in the shadows.

Christine cried the entire way home, stunned by what could have happened and baffled by her car's refusal to start the first time. The car had just been thoroughly inspected and had passed with flying colors.

She turned her thoughts toward God and thanked Him profusely for helping her out of what so easily might have been a life-threatening situation. She shuddered as she imagined what the man might have done if she had been stuck there just a few moments longer. Especially with the parking lot dark and most of the Christmas shoppers already gone.

She pulled into the driveway of their hillside home minutes later and, still feeling weak from the ordeal, made her way inside. There she tearfully shared the incident with her husband.

"You're safe now," Mike told her, taking her into his arms. After Christine had told him the specific details of the incident and what the man had looked like, Mike called the police. Once that was done, he turned to his wife.

"Let's go outside and look at the car," he said. "I can't understand why it would have done that. The mechanic just checked it out a few weeks ago, right?"

"Right," Christine said, nodding.

"I don't get it," Mike said, grabbing a flashlight and leading Christine outside toward the car. She watched as he opened the hood. Suddenly he stood back, allowing the flashlight to drop slowly by his side. He looked stunned, and Christine looked instantly concerned.

"What's wrong?" she asked.

"It's impossible," he muttered.

"What?" Christine moved closer, looking into the car's engine.

"There," Mike said, pointing the flashlight once more at the engine. "The battery is gone."

"What?" Christine was confused. "How could it be? I just got home."

Mike turned slowly toward his wife. "Don't you see? Someone set you up. While you were shopping, someone took your battery and then waited for you. They knew you wouldn't be able to start your car and..." Mike stopped mid-sentence imagining what the masked man had intended for his young, beautiful wife.

"It's impossible," he said again.

"I don't understand," Christine said. She was more confused than ever, and terrified at Mike's discovery. She had been set up and somehow escaped being attacked. "If the battery is gone, how did the car start, Mike?"

"That's what I mean. There isn't any way to start an engine like this without a battery."

Chills made their way down Christine's spine, and she reached for her husband's hand. "What are you saying?" she asked softly.

"I don't know. I can't explain it. Somehow you made it home without a battery. It's impossible."

Suddenly Christine felt a peace wash over her. "Mike, could it be God was watching out for me?"

Mike's eyes widened and a knowing look came over his face. Slowly, deliberately, he stared up at the star-covered sky. Christine followed his example, and for several minutes the couple gazed into the night. Finally, Mike broke the silence.

"God, we may never understand what happened tonight," he whispered. "But we are eternally grateful. Thank you."

Glimpse of a Guardian Angel

LL OF THE CHILDREN IN THE ROMAN FAMILY walked a straight and narrow path. Their parents, Candelario and Leonor, were born in Puerto Rico in the early part of the century. They had always taught their children to have self-respect, a kindness toward others, and a devotion to God. The Roman children grew up in the late 1950s and 1960s, in the borough of Manhattan in New York City on the Upper West Side, an area that at that time was often dangerous.

For that reason, the children had strict orders to come home immediately after school. One of the few places the children were allowed to play and participate in after-school activities was the Holy Name of Jesus Catholic Church on Ninety-sixth Street and Amsterdam Avenue. As a result, each of the eight Roman children grew up with a strong faith and a sense of morality that has lasted to this day.

Of all the Roman children, Linda, the youngest of the five girls, was perhaps the most devout. From a young age, she had a sense of responsibility and a desire to care for those who could not care for themselves. She was by her mother's standards the classic "good girl," and she grew up living what her family considered to be a charmed life. But there was something else that set Linda apart from her siblings. They believe Linda had a childhood guardian angel who made at least two appearances to her family members.

The first incident happened in 1966, when Linda was five years old. At that time, she slept in the same bedroom as two of her sisters, Carmen and Cookie, ages ten and twelve. The older girls did not mind sharing their space with Linda, because they felt it was their job to watch over her.

One night, long after the lights had been turned out and Linda had fallen asleep, Carmen and Cookie were still whispering to each other when they thought they heard something. Looking up, they glanced at Linda, and there, lying in her bed beside her, was a little girl of about the same age. For nearly a minute, the girls stared at the stranger in Linda's bed, exchanging looks of surprise, unsure what to do next.

Suddenly, the older girls slipped back under the covers, afraid that perhaps they were seeing a ghost or that if they turned away the strange little girl might become a monster. Eventually, Linda's frightened older sisters fell asleep, snuggled together under their bed covers. In the morning the little girl was gone, and Carmen and Cookie were baffled.

"Mommy," Carmen approached their mother before breakfast that morning, "Linda had a little girl sleeping with her last night and today she's gone."

The children's mother paused for a moment, wiped her hands on her apron, and looked thoughtfully at her daughter. "What do you mean, honey?"

"Last night me and Cookie were awake and we looked over at Linda's bed. There was a little girl sleeping right beside her. This morning she's gone. Who was she?"

Her mother paused again and tilted her head. Then she smiled. "I guess it was her guardian angel," she said.

Linda woke up shortly after and joined her family in the kitchen. Although only five years old, Linda knew instantly that her family was talking about her. When she asked her mother what her sisters were discussing, Leonor took the girl aside quietly.

"It's nothing to be scared about, honey," her mother said gently. "The girls saw an angel near your bed last night."

Linda thought about her mother's words for a moment and then nodded in understanding. "A good angel, Mommy?" she asked.

"Of course," her mother answered.

Although neither she nor anyone else in the Roman family knew why Linda might have needed a guardian angel, with the constant dangers of the inner city, the angel's presence was more comforting than curious. After that neither Linda nor her mother gave much thought to the incident. For Leonor, it was almost as if, in her deep faith, she was not terribly surprised that an angel might be watching over her children. Carmen and Cookie, however, talked about Linda's angel often, telling the story to their brothers and sisters on a regular basis and checking in on her at night in hopes that they would see the angel once more.

But years passed before the mysterious little girl was seen again. This time, Linda was a junior at a private girls' high school near their New York City apartment. By then, Linda had grown up quite close to her youngest brother, Joey. Each day at 3:30 p.m. Joey would wait anxiously in anticipation of his sister's return from school. Then the two would play together, listening to the radio and sharing secrets for hours. One afternoon. Linda's mother looked through the peephole of their apartment door and saw that Linda had just gotten off the elevator and was heading toward the door with a friend in tow.

"Joey, Linda's coming. She's got a friend with her," she yelled toward the back of the apartment, where Joey had been in his room playing.

The twelve-year-old boy came running at full speed toward the front door. He grabbed the nearest chair and stood up, looking through the peephole just as his mother had done minutes earlier.

Walking with Linda was a young girl who appeared to be sixteen or seventeen, the same age as Linda. She was dressed in the same school uniform and she seemed extraordinarily happy. Joey had never seen the girl before, and something about her brilliant blond hair caused him to stare. Then, as if she could sense his eyes on her, the girl darted playfully behind Linda, peeking her head out every few steps.

Joey climbed down from the chair, unlocked the apartment door, and waited as Linda opened it. Joey strained to look behind his sister but the blond girl had disappeared. Linda was all by herself.

"Hey, where's your friend?" Joey asked, suddenly confused as he stepped out into the hallway and peered up and down its length.

Linda looked strangely at her younger brother. "What friend?"

"You know, the girl who was with you. Where did she go? Come on, Linda!"

Linda shrugged, walking past Joey and putting her books down on the kitchen table. "I walked home by myself."

Joey caught up to his sister, took hold of her arm and turned her to face him. "This isn't funny, Linda. She was walking right beside you. Then she moved behind you, kind of like she was playing around or something. She had long blond hair and she had the same uniform as you. Where is she?"

At that moment Leonor walked into the room. "Where's your girlfriend, Linda?" she asked simply.

Linda wrinkled her face in confusion. "What girlfriend? I came home by myself."

"But I saw her..." Leonor's voice trailed off and she appeared to be deep in thought. There was silence for a moment. "There wasn't anyone with you?"

"No one, Mom."

The confusion in her face disappeared instantly. "Your guardian angel," she said plainly, having reached what was for her an obvious conclusion. She smiled at Linda and turned back toward the kitchen, where she had been preparing dinner.

Like the first time, when Carmen and Cookie had seen the strange little girl sleeping alongside their sister, Leonor never mentioned the incident again. Even Linda rarely talked about the times her family had seen the mysterious girl by her side. Now, at age thirty-seven, Linda still has never seen the girl she believes to be her guardian angel.

"But I have always had a special feeling of protection," says Linda, now happily married and with two beautiful children. "As if I knew for sure that God was looking out for me."

As for Joey, at thirty-two he remains baffled by the experience that afternoon, an event that has strengthened his faith and given him direction in life.

"I know I saw someone with Linda that day," he says. "Can she have been anyone but a guardian angel?"

A Message of Hope

THE MARKET COLORS BEGAN CHANGING while Jim Marlin was shopping for groceries. He had promised his family that he was finished with drugs. But in the San Fernando Valley of Southern California, where he lived, drugs were so easily accessible that he had once again been unable to resist. He had taken a mixture of illegal drugs hours earlier, and now, suddenly, the walls of the market seemed to be melting, their colors running into each other.

Jim looked around desperately, trying to steady himself, and aware that sweat had begun pouring from his forehead, dripping down his face, neck, and arms.

"Not now," he whispered out loud. "Please not now."

He turned toward the produce section, but the fruits and vegetables had turned into large bloblike substances, and worse, they were coming toward him.

"Help!" he screamed and began running full speed through the store, up one aisle and down the next. Finally, alerted by concerned customers, the store manager and one of the customers, a strong, well-built man in his late twenties, caught Jim and forced him to the ground.

"Hold his feet," the customer said calmly, directing the store manager toward Jim's legs. "I've got his arms."

In the middle of a terrible drug-induced hallucination, Jim writhed violently on the floor trying to free himself from the grasp of the men who held him down. The hallucination was getting worse.

Every time Jim opened his eyes, he saw horrible, dark demons coming toward him. They had fierce expressions and fangs that dripped blood. There were small, evil demons floating near his face and laughing at him, and there were huge, monstrous demons circling him. Worse than the way they looked, the demons seemed to be emanating a sense of utter evil, a death and destruction that Jim was powerless to escape.

"Help me, someone help me," he shouted. "They're trying to kill me."

The customer, who had been holding Jim's arms, leaned in closer to him.

"You're going to be OK," he said in a voice that was soothing and clear. Despite Jim's severe hallucinations, he could hear the man and he began nodding.

"Help me!" he shouted again.

"Open your eyes, Jim," the customer said calmly in a voice only Jim could hear. He appeared to be unaware of the gathering of people that had encircled them. "Come on, Jim, you can trust me."

Jim opened his eyes slowly, then as the picture became clearer, his eyes grew wide in astonishment. The demons were still there, but they were retreating. And in the center of the picture was what appeared to be the face of Jesus Christ. Awestruck, Jim stopped twisting and struggling and suddenly grew calm.

As he stared, the image in the center of the picture began to speak. "Do you want to be free from the demons, Jim?" the voice of the Christlike image asked. "You need to decide."

Suddenly, Jim began to cry, and the crowd, which had grown even larger, watched as the young man continued to lean over him, talking in a voice none of them could hear.

"Yes," Jim cried softly. "Help me get rid of the demons. Please, help me!"

The man in the picture smiled gently. "No more drugs, Jim. With them come the demons. It is your choice."

"No, I can't do it by myself," Jim screamed, and the people surrounding him and the customer who spoke to him began to fidget restlessly. There was something unreal about the conversation these two seemed to be having. Even though they still could not hear the quiet words of the man.

Jim had closed his eyes again and once more started to struggle out of the stranger's grasp. But the man seemed to possess an inhuman strength, and Jim's efforts were futile.

"Look at me, Jim," the gentle voice said again. "Trust me."

Slowly, Jim opened his eyes again. This time the demons were gone completely. Only the image of a very pure and radiant Christ filled the center of his vision.

"Help me," he whispered weakly. "Please."

"Jim, you won't have to do this by yourself. If you want to be rid of the demons, turn to me. I will always be right here to help you. Just call me and I will be with you."

"Lord?" Jim whispered the word, not sure if he was still hallucinating, but savoring the peace he felt all the same.

Slowly the image began to fade. But before it disappeared altogether, he heard the voice once more. "Yes, Jim. It is I. I will be here for you."

Suddenly Jim felt extremely tired. He closed his eyes and his body went limp. The customer who had been talking quietly to Jim and holding down his arms stood up.

"I think you can handle it from here," he said softly. "The worst of it is over."

"Thanks," the manager said, moving quickly toward Jim's arms and pinning the sleeping man down in case he awoke again. When the manager looked around to ask the customer what he had done to calm the man, the customer had vanished. At that moment, paramedics arrived and the manager stepped back so they could begin working. The police had also arrived, and the commotion was growing by the moment.

"Excuse me," a woman said as she made her way to Jim. "I'm his wife. Please let me see him."

Jim's wife, Jennika, a pretty, dark-haired woman with tears in her eyes, moved next to Jim and watched as paramedics took his vital signs.

"Seems to be OK now," one of them said. "Drug hallucination?" he asked, staring at the store manager.

"Yes, definitely. Never seen anything like it."

Jennika closed her eyes and began crying again. Jim had promised her his days of doing drugs were behind him. He had been in and out of a rehabilitation center twice in the past two years, and she was beginning to wonder if he would ever quit. The paramedics had backed away from Jim, having determined that he needed no immediate medical attention. As they moved away, Jennika moved in close to Jim's head.

"Jim, sweetheart, wake up," she whispered. "Come on, get up, honey."

Immediately Jim opened his eyes. "Where is he?" he asked.

Jennika was confused. "Who?"

Jim sat straight up and looked around until he saw the manager. "Where did he go, that man who was holding me down?"

The manager glanced at the crowd, which had dwindled to just a few people. "I guess he's gone."

Slowly, Jim rose to his feet. At that instant, a policeman moved in and placed handcuffs on Jim's wrists as he read him his rights. Because his hallucination had happened in a public place, the police were arresting him for making a public disturbance. In addition, they were concerned for his safety and the safety of those customers around him.

Before the police led him away, Jim turned again to the manager. "Please," he said, suddenly much calmer than he had been moments earlier during the hallucination. "Tell me what that man looked like."

The manager squirmed uncomfortably at the strange request. "He was, well," the manager began, trying to remember. "He had short blond hair, muscular build and, let's see, well, a real clean-shaven face. That's all I can remember."

Jim shook his head. "No, I mean the other man. The one who leaned over me and talked to me."

"Yes, that's who I'm telling you about."

"No, the man who helped me. He had dark hair, a beard, brown eyes. Where is he?"

The manager did not know what to make of Jim's statement. He had no experience with hallucinogenic drugs and no way of knowing what Jim had seen during the violent episode.

"All I can tell you is that the man who helped you was a blond guy," the manager said.

Jennika had been listening to the exchange between her husband and the store manager and was very curious about what Jim had seen and heard during his hallucination.

"Are you alright, Jim?" she asked.

Jim looked from the manager to his wife in frustration. "No one knows where he went?" he asked.

"No. He left right after you calmed down," the manager said. "Look, let's get this thing cleaned up. I've got a store to run here."

The policeman nodded and led Jim outside to the waiting police car.

"Something happened in there," he said, looking into his wife's eyes as he was ushered into the car. "My life will never be the same again, Jennika."

He saw the frightened look on her face, unsure of what to make of his statement.

"Don't worry, love," he said, smiling through tears. "I'll tell you everything later."

Jim was booked and released from the police station after promising to appear in court to deal with his public disturbance charge. Jennika picked him up at the station later that afternoon. Normally after he'd gotten into trouble because of his drug use, Jim was angry and defiant. But as Jennika watched him approach their car and climb inside, she saw that he was strangely upbeat.

"Are you going to tell me what happened back at the grocery store?" she asked, making no move to start the car and giving Jim her full attention.

"Yes," he said, staring out the window at the blue sky above. He turned toward Jennika. "Jen, do you believe God might be trying to tell me something?" he asked.

Jennika sighed. She was dying to know what had happened in the market, and Jim seemed bent on delaying the discussion.

"Of course," she answered patiently. Jennika was a prayerful Christian who asked God daily to help Jim stop doing drugs. Lately she had prayed that he would use whatever means necessary to reach Jim and help him to give his life over to God.

"Now please tell me what happened at the market," she begged.

"I'm not sure you're going to believe me, but I'll tell you. I did some drugs earlier and then I went shopping. Just had the munchies I guess," he began. "Then I began to hallucinate, everything was turning different colors and it seemed like the vegetables were coming to life." Jim glanced at his wife and was relieved to see that she wasn't laughing. She had never found any humor in his hallucinations, only disgust and sadness that they had been brought on by his drug use.

"Well, I began sweating and then I think I started running through the store screaming for help," he said. Jennika's eyes narrowed in pain, sorry she hadn't been near her husband to help him. "Well, I began to see black beings in the air and I closed my eyes. I think I just stood there screaming for help. When I opened my eyes, there were demons; that's the only way I can describe them. They were all around me—black beings with fangs and claws and blood dripping from their mouths. Oh, Jennika, it was so horrible."

Jim hung his head for a moment, reliving the nightmare of the hallucination. Jennika reached over and took his hand.

"Honey, tell me what happened next."

Jim nodded. "Well, I felt someone grab me and then someone was holding my feet and someone else was holding my arms. I had my eyes closed and I was still screaming. Then, all of a sudden I can hear this calm, gentle voice telling me to open my eyes and to trust him. Now, here's where it gets really weird. I opened my eyes slowly and the demons were leaving, they were moving away as fast as they could. And in the center of the picture was a man who looked exactly like the pictures of Christ I've seen. He was holding my arms gently and speaking softly so that only I could hear him."

"Did he say anything?" Jennika asked, mesmerized by the story Jim was telling.

"Yes," Jim nodded again. "He told me that if I wanted to get rid of the demons I would have to stop the drugs. Then he told me he would help me so I wouldn't have to do it on my own."

"That's all?"

"Well, after that I felt a lot of peace. The demons had gone completely, and I sort of fell asleep for a few moments. When I woke up, I wanted to talk to the man. Whoever he was, he had held me in place and talked to me. But he was gone. The manager didn't know where he'd gone."

"You mean the manager saw him, too?" Jennika asked.

"Yes, I guess everyone must have seen him. There were quite a few people standing around when all this was happening."

"And no one saw where he went?"

"No. But you want to know what's the weirdest thing of all?"

Jennika already felt funny about Jim's story, but she nodded.

"Well, I asked the manager what the man looked like who was bending over me, talking to me and holding my arms down. You know what he said? He told me the man had blond hair and was clean shaven. But that's not what I saw when I opened my eyes. I saw Jesus Christ. I mean it, Jennika. That's the only way I can describe him. He was talking to me very softly, and I knew he had come to warn me. If I don't change things now, with His help, the demons will get me. I believe that's why he appeared to me like that."

"But what about the blond guy? Was he talking to you or was some image in your hallucination?"

"I'm not sure. But everyone saw the man who held me down talking to me. They just couldn't hear what he said."

"So you think it was a warning?" Jennika asked tentatively. She had prayed that Jim's life would be drastically changed, but she had never expected this type of answer from the Lord.

"Yes. And I'm telling you now that I will never touch drugs again, Jennika. I am going to turn to God and give Him a proper place in my life. I don't want His message to be in vain."

"Hmmm," Jennika said. "That's interesting."

"What?"

"Message. You were given a message from God. Do you know how messages from God were delivered in biblical times?"

Jim shook his head.

"From angels, Jim," she said slowly. "Maybe the man who was talking to you was an angel, telling you what the Lord wanted you to hear."

Jim thought a moment. "I don't know, Jen," he said after a while. "I guess we never will know who was really talking to me, who the messenger was. But I'm going to heed the message. I know that for sure."

Jim made several follow-up phone calls to the supermarket in search of the man who had helped him that afternoon. But the manager apparently never saw the man again. He had been available, helped in an emergency situation, and then disappeared. But not in vain.

Jim kept his word. For the next twenty years and still today, Jim Marlin has stayed away from all drugs and worked each year on making his marriage to Jennika better than ever. He has also maintained a dynamic relationship with God, one that began on a cold supermarket floor in the grasp of a man who was, perhaps, an angel.

Angelic Reassurance

∾

I T WAS THE SUMMER OF 1982, and Ann Holman and Linda Rust had been planning a trip for months. Their husbands and sons had been vacationing together at Lake Powell, boating and fishing for the past week. Now, on an early Saturday morning in Canoga Park, California, Ann and Linda were about to take their three small daughters and drive eight hours to Sedona, Arizona, where they would meet up with the men.

"Be sure to have the station wagon checked before you leave," Harley Rust had told his wife earlier that week. "You don't want to break down in the desert with those little girls."

Linda agreed. She took the wagon to a local mechanic's shop and had a complete tune-up done.

"Everything looks great, Mrs. Rust," the mechanic assured her. "Belts are fine, fluids are fine. Shouldn't have any trouble on the trip."

Linda thanked the man, and by Friday afternoon she and Ann were busy packing the wagon with things they would need for a long drive. Early Saturday morning, before the sun came up, the women and their children set out toward the desert on Interstate 10. They stopped in Indio for gasoline, and a local mechanic offered to check under the hood. After several minutes of intensely scrutinizing the engine, the mechanic straightened himself and shook his head in concern.

"Doesn't look good, ladies," he said ominously.

Linda moved closer to the car and stared at the engine. "What's wrong?"

"Fan belt's going," he said. "Might not snap for another hundred miles or so. Of course, if it snaps while you're driving, it could be dangerous."

Linda wrinkled her brow and motioned for Ann to join her. "He says the fan belt looks ready to snap and it could be dangerous," she told her friend and then turned back to the mechanic. "What could happen?" she asked.

"Well, not always, but sometimes the force will send it right through the hood and the windshield. Right into the passenger area."

Linda shuddered at the thought of the outcome if the fan belt flew into the area where the children were sitting. "What if we replaced it?" she asked.

"Of course, that would be the safest thing to do," he said slowly. "Cost about $300."

Linda was silent a moment, weighing the man's words. "We need to think it over," she said, dismissing the man and pulling Ann closer to her. "What do you think?"

"You just had the car checked," Ann said. "Don't you think your own mechanic would have told you if there'd been a problem with the fan belt?"

Linda nodded. "Maybe he's just trying to take us for $300. Here we are in the middle of nowhere, a couple of women and a bunch of little girls. What do we know?"

Ann pursed her lips and stared into the engine area. "I wish we knew more. I don't have any idea where the fan belt is or what it's supposed to look like."

"Me neither. What should we do?"

"Whatever you think. It's your car," Ann said, patting her friend on the back.

"OK. Let's pray for safety and drive on to Blythe. That's another two hours, and we'll see what happens. We can get another opinion at a garage there."

Ann nodded, rounded up the girls, and strapped them into the car. Immediately she began praying, asking God for safety and discernment. If the belt was about to go, she prayed for a sign so that they would have the wisdom to pull over before anyone got hurt.

Prayer was nothing new for Ann and Linda. The women and their families had met while attending West Valley Christian Church in West Hills. Ann and Linda had learned to incorporate their faith into everything they did.

As Linda started the station wagon, she prayed aloud that God would guide them safely to Blythe and keep the car from breaking down until they were near a gas station. Even the little girls joined in the prayer.

"Please keep us safe, Jesus," seven-year-old Joy added from the backseat.

The next two hours passed slowly as the women remained silent, both continuing to pray as they drove. Despite their faith, there was tension in the air as they continued. When they were only a few miles from Blythe, the children needed to use a bathroom, and the women decided to turn off at a rest area a mile up the interstate. The stop was situated on a flat piece of desert land with an empty parking lot that circled a small hut in the center. Pulling into the deserted rest station, Linda parked the car and sent the girls toward the bathrooms. Then she lifted the hood of her wagon.

"Come here, Ann," she said. "Let's take a look at the engine. If it's getting worse, maybe we'll be able to see it now."

Ann joined her, and the women bent over and looked closely at the various engine parts, completely unaware of what they were looking at. Eventually they stood up, still staring at the engine and trying to distinguish one part from another and hoping to locate the fan belt. Suddenly they heard a voice.

"Can I help?"

The women turned to see an unassuming Hispanic man standing directly behind them. He was dressed in jeans and a blue, button-down shirt, and he had dark hair and eyes. He smiled warmly, standing back a bit so as to not frighten the women. Still, they were startled at first, since they had not heard him walk up and did not see any other cars in the area. But the women were put at ease by something in the man's eyes, a gentleness they could not describe. Ann and Linda stepped aside, motioning for the man to take a look at the engine.

"A mechanic in Indio told us the fan belt was ready to snap," Linda explained. "But honestly, we don't know what we're looking for."

The man smiled and moved closer to the car. For several minutes he looked at the engine, touching various parts and looking thoroughly at others. Finally, he stepped back and gazed directly into Linda's eyes, then Ann's.

"The car is fine," he said clearly and deliberately, much the way a parent would talk to children. "There are no mechanical problems at all. Relax and enjoy your trip."

The women nodded and moved once more toward the engine, peering in at the parts, all of which still appeared foreign to them. At that moment they both realized how tense they had been for the past two hours. Although they had been praying constantly and believed that God would take care of them, they had not enjoyed the trip. Linda smiled and turned to thank the man for his reassurance.

But the man was gone.

"Hey, where'd he go?" Linda asked and Ann turned around. There was no one anywhere near them.

"That's impossible," Ann said softly. "Where could he have gone?"

The women stood planted in place, scanning the grounds of the rest station. But the man in the blue shirt had disappeared.

For the next four hours the women drove on to Sedona without worrying about the car. Not until that evening did they discuss the man, his message, and his disappearance.

"After he told us everything was fine I just stopped worrying about it," Linda said.

Ann nodded. "Almost like he gave us a sense of peace, that there really wasn't anything wrong."

"Maybe God wanted us to know he had heard our prayers and we didn't need to be concerned about car trouble," Linda said, looking at her friend and speaking matter-of-factly. "There was no way he could have gone anywhere that quickly, Ann. You know who he was, don't you?"

"Do you really think so?"

Linda nodded and smiled.

"An angel?"

"Is there any other explanation?"

Ann shook her head slowly. "Amazing, isn't it?"

"Amazing grace."

Heavenly Help in
the Emergency Room

T AGE EIGHT, Joey Clark had been in hospital emergency rooms numerous times, but none of them as serious as that summer morning in 1990. Betty, the boy's mother, sat in the emergency room alone, praying quietly.

"I can't promise anything," the doctor had told her. "I'm sorry, Mrs. Clark. It doesn't look like he's going to make it this time."

Joey had joined the Clark family when he was only a few months old. At that time, Betty and Dan Clark were licensed foster parents for the state of California in Los Angeles County. Joey came to them on a clear, windy day one winter in 1982, a tiny baby with dark hair, big eyes, and a very still body.

"He has numerous physical and mental handicaps," the social worker had explained to Dan and Betty. "He may not live through the week. I know it won't be easy, but I need to know if you can take him. His mother is unable to care for him, and he needs a safe place to stay."

Betty swallowed hard, trying to keep from crying before the tiny handicapped child.

"We'll do our best," Dan spoke up, taking the baby gently in his arms. "He'll be our little son for as long as you need us to take care of him."

The Clarks had two daughters, both of whom were well into their teenaged years and busy with their own lives. Joey would take more time than the other foster children they'd taken in, but the Clarks had always relied on their faith in trying times, and usually grew stronger in the process. Dan figured this situation would be one of those occasions. He prayed silently for the child's health, and listened carefully as the social worker discussed detailed directions for caring for the special child in his arms.

Joey lived through the week as the Clarks developed a routine around the needy infant. Six months later, despite his handicaps, Joey seemed to be thriving. Betty checked with the social worker and found that the boy's mother did not feel capable of caring for a child with such severe handicaps.

"You shouldn't have him much longer," she added. "We're trying to place him in a home or a facility where he can be cared for full time."

Betty was shocked. "He doesn't need to be in a facility!" she said, outraged at the idea. "He is a child. He needs love and a family to care for him."

The social worker sighed. "Yes, I know that, Mrs. Clark. But Joey's disabilities are so severe, he will need special care all his life. He will never speak or walk or even be able to feed himself."

"But he's a child, still," Betty responded. "He needs love more than he needs special care. Especially from an institute. We'll keep him here until you find a home for him."

The social worker agreed, but six months later she had still not found a permanent home for the little boy. Dan and Betty and their daughters celebrated the boy's first birthday and a few days later realized that the social worker was right. A home might never be found for the child they'd come to love as their own.

"I guess we have just one choice," Dan said one evening.

"The home is right here, isn't it?" Betty asked, tears filling her eyes as she smiled, knowing her husband felt the same way.

Dan nodded. "Let's look into it."

Over the next few months, the Clarks went through the necessary steps to take legal custody of the boy. In order to receive state financial assistance for Joey's medical needs, they could not adopt him. But he would now be their legal dependent, and in their eyes, he would be their son. When the procedure was final, the Clarks threw another birthday party for Joey and were thrilled to see his eyes show signs of responding.

Years passed and Joey continued to show delight in the attention he received. Although he was not born with the physical ability to sit, stand, or speak, Joey could make sounds and use his eyes to show emotion. When Joey was still very young, the Clarks were able to distinguish between Joey's expressions and knew when he was hungry, tired, or in need of extra attention. He would always need to be hand-fed through tubing, and he would never develop the independence of caring for himself. But the Clarks loved him with a fierce, protective love that brought deep meaning to their lives. Never did they regret adopting the boy or give any thought to the time and energy Joey required of them.

"I know he can't do the things another little boy might be able to do," Dan would say when people asked about Joey. "But he has his own accomplishments. And for how much he tries, I couldn't be prouder of him. I love him so much. More, probably, than I could have loved a child without his problems."

Illness was a part of Joey's life, a part that worried his parents often. Because he had so little control over his muscle function, Joey did not cough the way an able-bodied child would. For that reason, he often contracted respiratory infections, and several times in his young life he had been hospitalized for pneumonia and other life-threatening problems.

That was the case in the summer of 1990, when Joey had been hospitalized for pneumonia and released. But now, despite antibiotics, Joey had gotten much worse and he wasn't eating. Finally, in the hours after midnight, Betty was awakened by the sound of Joey gasping for air. She raced him to the nearest emergency room, but by then her son was barely breathing. Doctors had tried to put a tube in the boy's stomach to force-feed him, but they had not inserted it correctly, and now in addition to his infection he had food spilling into the cavity of his upper torso. His chances of surviving emergency surgery in his condition were very slim.

After the doctor's ominous diagnosis, Betty knew she had just one way to find peace. She found a quiet corner in the waiting room—which at 3 a.m. was completely empty—hung her head and began to pray.

"Lord," she prayed in a whispered voice. "Please help my little boy. I love him so, and I know he's scared right now. Please help him to breathe."

At that instant, Betty heard someone enter the room through the open door. She looked up and saw a small man dressed in janitorial clothing and pulling a mop and water bucket on wheels. Something about the man's face seemed unnaturally kind, and Betty stared at him curiously. His uniform was rumpled, and he seemed almost stooped in the humble demeanor of servant.

"I have something to tell you," the man said softly, looking directly at Betty. "A message from God."

Betty was taken aback by the man's statement. But she leaned forward so she could hear him better, never once feeling afraid of him. She waited as the man took one step closer and smiled gently.

"He's going to be OK," the man said. *"Malachi 4:2."*

Then, before Betty could ask him any of the dozens of questions that raced through her mind, the man turned around and left.

Betty stood up quickly and moved across the room toward the door. She stepped into the hallway expecting to see the man a few feet away, but he was gone. None of the other doors in the hallway were open. Betty couldn't imagine how he could have gotten away so quickly, especially pulling a bucket of water.

She waited a moment, looking up and down the hallway in both directions, hoping to see which way the man had gone. But after a while she turned around and moved slowly back to her seat. How had the man known about Joey? Could he possibly have known that she was waiting for news about whether her son would live through the night? And what did the Bible verse he had mentioned have to do with her situation? Donna was baffled as she considered the man's words.

Finally, she resolved to find the man and learn why he had told her everything was going to be all right and who had told him to tell her. She went up to the emergency check-in counter.

I need to speak with one of your hospital janitors," she said matter-of-factly. "He was small, about this tall," she used her hand to show how high the man had stood. "And he stopped by the waiting room here a few minutes ago. I'm not sure where he is right now, but I need to talk to him. Could you page him?"

The receptionist pulled out a schedule and scanned it slowly.

"That's what I thought," she said, her voice puzzled.

"What?"

"The janitors," she said, looking up from the paper and staring at Betty. "They've all gone home. They left three hours ago."

Betty shook her head. "No, there must be someone else, another janitor or something. The one I talked to walked right into that room," she pointed toward the waiting area. "I just saw him, not ten minutes ago. He's somewhere down that hallway."

"Well, all I can tell you, ma'am, is he doesn't work at this hospital. Our janitors went home. They're all off the clock. Besides, I don't think we even have a janitor that fits the description you gave me."

Betty stepped backward and turned around, moving slowly toward the sofa in the waiting room. She was still trying to understand who the man might have been, when Joey's doctor walked into the room.

"Well, Mrs. Clark. I have to say it's nothing short of a miracle," the doctor said, breaking into a smile. "Joey wasn't breathing well at all. In fact, ten minutes ago we thought we were losing him. Then he suddenly began coughing, and in a few minutes he was breathing normally again. I can't explain it."

"He's OK, then?" Betty asked, fresh tears filling her eyes as she rose to meet the doctor.

"He's still sick, but the danger's passed."

Joey went home two days later, but Betty never forgot how close she and Dan came to losing their son that morning. The Bible verse, *Malachi* 4:2, talked about revering God's name so that healing would come. She always kept the verse with her after that and found herself reciting it numerous times as she and Joey faced the trials that came with his condition. But no matter how sick Joey became, she never forgot the small man in the janitorial uniform who delivered what she knows was an angelic message of hope.

"God used that man, whoever he was, to reassure me that Joey was going to be all right. My prayers had been heard."

The Vanishing Prison Guard

OHN MARK WAS HANDSOME AND CAREFREE, twenty-five years old and at a crossroads. Raised in a God-fearing home, he knew he had strayed away from his upbringing. But recently he had begun to experiment with drugs and a faster lifestyle, which threatened to destroy his chances to ever turn back. He was in college, but without any particular direction in life. He sometimes wondered what point there was in working so hard for an uncertain future.

These were his thoughts one night in 1982 as he drove along the Florida Turnpike. Why not, he told himself, give in to the pressures around him? At least the parties he'd been attending—and the drugs he'd been doing—gave him some satisfaction. Even if it was temporary.

The longer Mark thought about his situation, the more he began to believe that he should drop out of college. Life would be simpler, something seemed to be telling him, if he weren't so burdened with responsibilities.

"And the last thing I need to get messed up with right now is church," he mumbled out loud, peering straight ahead into the dark Florida night. That had been his mother's suggestion, but he had rebelled against the idea since first hearing it. "Never helped me any before," he'd told her. "Can't help me much now."

Mark drove on until, suddenly, he spotted what looked like a fully dressed prison guard hitchhiking along the side of the road. Mark had never picked up a hitchhiker, but something about the man suggested he was on the way to work and genuinely in need of a ride. Mark pulled over and rolled down his window. The man stooped down and looked inside, smiling.

"Need a ride?" Mark asked tentatively.

"Thanks, I was hoping you'd stop," he said, each word carefully measured. "Car's broken down."

Mark nodded in understanding and opened his car door. He hadn't seen any broken-down cars alongside the roadway, but the man seemed kind enough. Mark was not afraid that his hitchhiking might be some kind of ruse to rob or harm him.

Mark glanced at his passenger and saw that the man was well into his fifties, with graying hair and a moustache. He had kind, blue eyes and a face that seemed filled with light. His prison guard uniform was perfectly pressed, and he seemed strangely out of place in it.

"You a prison guard?" Mark asked, picking up speed and resuming his drive along the highway.

The man nodded. "Just got off work. State penitentiary back down the road a ways." There was only one such prison in the vicinity and Mark knew the place.

"What's your name?"

"Kenneth. Kenneth Hawes. Worked at the prison for the past ten years."

Mark was silent a moment. "I have a long drive ahead of me. Where are you going?" Mark noticed that the man seemed unusually calm and relaxed, considering he was with a stranger in an unfamiliar car after a breakdown of his own.

"Home," he said softly, smiling at Mark as if home were the most wonderful place in the world. "About an hour up the road. Now, why don't you tell me what's on your mind?"

Mark was unsure what to make of the man, but he shrugged and started telling him his age and what he was studying in school.

"No," the man said softly. "Tell me about the crossroad."

Mark stared at the man, wondering how he could have known to ask such a question.

"What?" he asked.

"You know what I mean. You have some choices you're trying to make, don't you?"

Mark felt strangely uncomfortable, as if the man could somehow read his thoughts. But he shrugged once again, convincing himself that the man could not possibly have known anything about his personal life. The stranger was only lonely and looking for conversation.

"Yeah, I know what you mean," he said. With a loud sigh, Mark decided to tell the man the truth. He told him about his upbringing and how his parents prayed for him daily.

"But I'm different now, that kind of life is in my past," Mark said, waving his hand as if to indicate he would never again involve himself in organized religion.

"No," the man's voice was sudden and firm. Mark looked at him; he was shaking his head. "It's closer than you think."

"You're a prison guard, what would you know?" Mark asked, suddenly irritated with this strange man's intrusive comments.

"I do know," he said. The man's answer was not defensive or angry, but he spoke with a finality that set Mark on edge.

"Well, that's about it. I have a couple ways I could go and it looks like I'm taking the one that fits me best. Forget school, forget religion. Forget everything."

The man said nothing. He stared straight ahead for several minutes before turning again toward Mark. "Mark, you know there's only one way, don't you?"

"Look, thanks for listening but I'm tired of talking. My exit is coming up. Where can I drop you off?"

The man smiled, his attitude unchanged by Mark's brusqueness. With a series of directions, he led Mark to a busy intersection. "This is close enough, Mark."

"Listen, I can take you to your house. Really. It's too late to be walking home alone out here."

"I can find my home from here," he said, shaking his head firmly and turning to face Mark squarely. "Make the right choice, son. Now. You still have the chance, you know."

He climbed out, shut the door and waved once before turning away and walking up the street. For a moment Mark wanted to follow him, to spend more time talking with him and to glean something from the wisdom he seemed to possess. But the night was late and he had school in the morning. He pulled his car back onto the main road and headed back toward the turnpike.

Through the night and into the next morning Mark thought over everything the man had said. How had he known so much? And why would he have been hitchhiking home when he lived so far from the prison? Finally Mark decided he needed to talk to the man once more. He called the prison from his dormitory that afternoon.

"I'd like to speak to Kenneth Hawes," Mark said. "He's a prison guard."

There was a pause on the other end. "I don't believe he works here."

Mark furrowed his eyebrows. "Of course he works there. He was working yesterday evening, and I gave him a ride home. He had his uniform on and everything."

"Well, sir, I can let you talk with my supervisor, but to my knowledge there isn't any prison guard named Kenneth Hawes at this facility."

"Fine," Mark said, and he could feel his frustration rising. "Let me talk to your supervisor."

The supervisor spent ten minutes convincing Mark that there wasn't now and never had been a Kenneth Hawes employed at the prison. At Mark's request, she also checked the other prison facilities in the state but none of them employed a Kenneth Hawes either.

Stunned, Mark hung up the phone. The man had ridden with him for more than an hour, giving him advice about his life and trying to point him in the right direction. Now he had disappeared, almost as if he had never existed.

Frustrated and wanting to share the story, Mark called his mother that evening and told her what had happened.

"Sometimes God gets our attention in interesting ways," his mother said quietly. "Did you ever think that he might have been an angel?"

"An angel? Like in the Bible stories?" Mark asked doubtfully.

"Why not? God is still God, and His ways aren't so different now than in Bible times," she said.

For several weeks Mark considered the possibility until, finally, he was convinced that his mother was right. Kenneth must have been an angel sent to guide him through a time in his life when he had crucial choices to make. How better for God to get his attention than with a prison guard, especially in light of the choices he'd been making lately.

Almost overnight, Mark decided he would no longer involve himself in harmful activities, such as drugs and all-night parties. Instead, over the next year he doubled his efforts toward school and began attending church again. In the process, he found a peace and assurance he had never believed could exist. Eventually, Mark earned a degree in telecommunications and went on to serve as a news reporter for one of the television news shows in southern Florida.

More than a decade later, he is as certain as ever that God used an angel to change his life.

Heavenly Visitor

USSELL JOHNSON'S THIRD HEART ATTACK happened on the job. As captain of the Wayne, Michigan, fire department, Russell didn't need to don a uniform and fight fires any more, especially after his two recent heart attacks. But on a warm day in 1974, Russell couldn't resist. He was in the heat of battling a raging fire when the pain struck.

"Help!" he shouted as loudly as he could above the roar of the fire.

One of the firefighters nearby heard him and summoned help. Together they carried him out of the burning building, and paramedics rushed him to the hospital. When the danger had passed, Russell took the only choice the doctors were giving him if he wanted to live. He retired.

Having raised four daughters, Russell and his wife, Jean, decided to move to Punta Gorda, Florida, where they bought a small home and began living the life of retirees. Although they had very little money, they found enjoyment in the regular visits they received from their four daughters and their families. Russell also set up a workshop in his garage, where he spent hours repairing church organs and making dollhouses.

One afternoon in November 1985, Russell, now sixty-five years old, was tinkering out in his workshop, making tiny shingles for a dollhouse he was building, when there was a knock on the front door. Moments later Jean entered the shop, her face ghostly white.

"There's a huge man at the door," she said, her voice barely more than a whisper. "He's dressed in rags and I don't know what to do. He's waiting there."

Russell set down his tools on the workbench and led the way back into the house. From the peephole in the front door, Russell could see his wife was right. The man was possibly six feet five inches and easily weighed 275 pounds. He was a mountain of a man, dirty, and wearing torn clothes. He carried a small satchel. Russell opened the door and smiled.

"Can I help you, sir?"

The man lowered his eyes humbly and cleared his throat. "Yes, I was wondering if you might have some work I could do in exchange for some food."

Russell was struck by the man's gentle personality. As he and Jean stood looking at the man filling their doorway, they were suddenly no longer afraid of the man.

"Well," Russell said slowly, "I haven't got any work for you. But we can sure get you something to eat."

The man looked up, and his eyes seemed to glimmer with a new sense of hope. Jean turned and headed toward the kitchen.

"I don't know how I can thank you kind people," he said. "See, I'm from Texas, got caught up in the oil crunch and thought I could find work if I headed out here."

Russell nodded his understanding. "You look pretty tired," he said. "Can I get you something to rest on?"

"Yes, in fact I am pretty tired. Been walking much of the day. I'd appreciate a chair."

Russell went out back and brought back three folding chairs. He set them up on the driveway and joined the man outside. The large man seemed very tired and thankful for the place to sit. For several minutes, the men sat together in a comfortable silence.

As Russell watched the stranger, he wondered what terrible twists the man's life had taken to bring him to the place of begging for food. He and Jean had never known a time where there wasn't food on the table or a roof over their heads. But in recent years, their finances had become very tight; he could only imagine how terrible it would be to have no home and no idea where one's next meal was coming from.

The day before, Russell remembered, he and his wife had taken a trip to the market and carefully bought food for the week, spending all the money they had until their next pension check later that month.

Russell was certain that Jean understood the hasty way he had agreed to feed the man. Even though they had precious little, they had more than this poor man. Russell was suddenly overwhelmed with thankfulness. The good Lord had always provided them with all they needed. Now he was glad to help this stranger, even if it was only by providing the man with a meal.

Jean finished making a plate of sandwiches and brought it outside with a pitcher of iced tea. The man thanked her and then hungrily began eating. He finished four sandwiches and several large glasses of iced tea before wiping his mouth and standing to leave.

"That was perfect," he said. "You don't know how thankful I am."

"Let me go back in the house and pack you a dinner," Jean said, turning and heading toward the front door. Russell smiled. He and Jean thought alike. He had been about to suggest the same thing. Russell turned back toward the man.

"Sir, have you got any money on you?" Russell asked curiously.

"Why, yes, I have thirteen cents," the man answered, his voice ringing with honesty.

"Stay right here," Russell said. "I'll be right back."

Russell went into the house and found a dollar in his billfold. Then he began scrounging through the family sugar bowl which always contained loose change. He managed to find five dollars, which he carefully carried outside. Jean had already joined the man by then and was handing him a sack dinner. She described the bag's contents and apologized that she couldn't provide him with anymore for the next day. Russell stepped forward.

"Here." Russell held the money out to the man. "Maybe this will help you get through another day or so a little bit easier."

The man took the money and placed it carefully in his satchel. Then he looked up at Russell and Jean.

"You people have been so kind to me," he said, his eyes moist. "Thank you." He paused a moment as if searching for something else to say. "Thank you."

He turned away, walking toward the sidewalk. When he reached the bottom of their driveway, he turned to face them and raised his hand in what appeared to be almost a salute.

"God bless you!" he said, his voice filled with emotion. "And thank you."

Then he turned and walked the length of the Johnson's corner house and turned right, heading along the side of their house and backyard toward the freeway, a few blocks away.

The Johnsons headed back into the house, shaken by the man's thankfulness. It had felt wonderful to help someone who was far needier than they had ever been. Indeed, as their preacher had often said, there had been a true blessing in giving. As he walked into the house, Russell immediately made his way into the backyard to resume work in his workshop. As he did, he leaned over the fence to say a final goodbye to the man, who by then should have been passing along the side of their backyard.

But the man had disappeared.

There were no bushes or trees or places to hide. Russell calculated the time he had taken to walk from the front yard into the back. Seven seconds or less, he figured. They had seen the man walking along the sidewalk that bordered the right side of their property. He was heading toward the freeway, which meant he would have to walk along the edge of their backyard and beyond. Yet somehow, in only a few seconds, the man had disappeared. Russell stood rooted in place. How could the man have disappeared like that?

"Jean," he called. "Come here."

Jean walked outside. "What is it?"

"That man, wasn't he walking this way?"

"Yes." Jean pointed toward their side fence. "If you look, you should be able to see him walking toward the freeway."

Russell shook his head. "He's gone, Jean. Nowhere."

Jean furrowed her eyebrows and joined her husband next to their fence. He was right. The man had disappeared. For the next fifteen minutes, Jean and Russell scoured the sidewalks that ran in front of and beside their corner house. Finally, they asked Joe, who lived across the street. Russell liked to say that Joe knew how many sparrows came and went through the neighborhood on a given day. Certainly he would know which way the man had gone.

The Johnsons found Joe sitting in his outdoor rocker sipping lemonade, which was how Joe typically spent his afternoons and early evenings. Russell described the large man who had visited their home and his haggard appearance.

"Haven't seen him at all," Joe said. "You sure he was by your place today?"

"Of course we're sure," Russell said, pointing across the street at his own driveway. "The wife fixed him a bunch of sandwiches. Sat right out there and ate 'em."

"That's strange," Joe said. "I've been home all day. Didn't see anyone over at your house. Guess I can't help you."

Discouraged at what had become of the man and what his fate might be with so little food and money, Russell and Jean decided to head back into their home. For several minutes, the two sat in their living room in silence, each wondering about the man who had shared lunch with them and how he had disappeared so quickly.

"Something special about the man, don't you think, Russell?" Jean asked softly.

"Something very special. Guess we'll never know who he was or what might become of him. I just wish there had been something else we might have done."

Jean paused a moment. "What if he was an angel?"

Russell chuckled lightly. "Come on, you're not serious are you? Angels don't dress like that."

"Yes," Jean insisted. "You remember the Bible verse about being careful to entertain strangers, for by doing so, some have entertained angels without knowing it? Well, what if he was that kind of stranger?"

Russell thought for a moment. He and Jean had not been regular church attenders in recent years, but they still considered themselves strong believers.

"I guess it sounds familiar," Russell said slowly. "So, you think this was some kind of test or something?"

"I don't know," Jean said, smiling and taking her husband's hand. "I keep thinking of that scripture that says, 'Whatsoever you do for the least of these, you do unto Me.' Maybe that's why we feel so good about what happened and the small way in which we could help."

Jean was silent a moment and then continued. "Maybe the man wasn't an angel, maybe he was just a guy who was down on his luck," she said. "But I can't explain where the man went and neither can you."

After that, the Johnsons told no one about the strange man, his humble gratefulness and his sudden disappearance. But one month later, Jean was opening Christmas cards, when she grew suddenly and strangely silent.

"Russell," she said loudly, clearly distracted by the card she was holding. "Someone must be playing a practical joke on you."

Russell entered the kitchen. "What is it?" he asked, walking up to where she sat at the dining room table.

"This card," she held a simple Christmas card up for her husband to see. "It's signed, 'love from your Christian friend.' There's no return address."

"Let's see that," Russell said, taking the card.

"That's not all of it," she said, holding up a slip of paper. "This was inside."

Russell took the paper and stared at it. It was a cashier's check made out to the Johnsons for $500.

"Jean, this is no joke, this is a real legal-like check," Russell said, his eyes wide. "Who could have done such a thing?"

Jean shook her head, speechless. She was unable to imagine which of their friends might have been able to spare such a large amount of money. But it wasn't until the next year at Christmas time, when the Johnsons received a similar card with another cashier's check for $500 that they were struck by an idea.

"Do you think there could be some connection," Jean asked her husband that year, "between these cards and that man we helped?"

"I don't think we'll ever know. But I still say it felt better helping him out that day than it feels to get this money in the mail. Even though we certainly could use it."

For the next three years the Johnsons received a Christmas card from their mysterious Christian friend, accompanied by a $500 cashier's check. After that, the mysterious cards stopped coming. Only then did they share the story with their children.

"We were afraid they'd think we were crazy," says Russell, who saved each of the Christmas cards, the envelopes they came in, and copies of the cashier's checks. "This is one of those stories that seems hard to believe. But it's true. Every word."

Even now, Russell and Jean are not convinced the anonymous cards and cashier's checks are related to their helping a hungry stranger—and maybe even an angel—weeks before Christmas.

"We never had any thought of getting something back," Russell says. "That isn't what giving is all about."

The Boy and the Bus

ॐ

HERE WERE TIMES WHEN DR. MIKE BARNS wondered why he went into the medical profession. People were always complaining about one ailment or another, and none of them understood that he was a busy man. Very busy. The way his schedule had been for the past several years, he wondered how he had survived. There had been a time, long ago, when he had been involved in his church, active in his faith. But prayer and devotions took time—a precious commodity Dr. Barns no longer had. And so he had let those things that had once brought him such peace and joy pass from his life almost completely. By the world's standards, Dr. Barns, at twenty-nine years old, had everything anyone could ever want. Good looks, youth, more than enough money, and a successful career that placed him in a position of esteem among his peers.

He gave little thought to much of this as he raced his BMW across a two-lane Arizona desert highway toward Lake Tahoe, situated along the border between Nevada and California. The vacation would last less than a week, but for months Dr. Barns had been looking forward to getting away from his overwhelming responsibilities. He stared straight ahead, trying only to clear his mind and his body of the hectic pace it had become accustomed to.

Picking up his cellular telephone, he tried to make a call. An hour had passed since he'd checked in with his office exchange. Duty and a tendency to perfectionism, rather than love for his patients, drove him to worry constantly about the messages he was missing. He dialed the number but nothing happened. Angrily, he tapped the receiver on the steering wheel.

"Come on," he said, his teeth clenched.

He dialed again but still nothing happened. "Stupid machine," he muttered, glancing at the vast expanse of desert that surrounded him. "Supposed to work anywhere."

He glanced down at his speedometer and noticed he was driving twenty miles over the speed limit.

"Just can't slow down, can you, Barns?" he said aloud, laughing bitterly and forcing himself to slow his pace and savor the solitude of the drive.

At that moment he saw a small figure ahead, on the side of the highway. Barns took his foot off the gas pedal and coasted, scanning the highway ahead and behind him for a broken-down car. There was none. He was getting closer to the figure, and he realized it was a small boy, dressed in scouting gear and wearing a red baseball cap. The boy was waving at him frantically, motioning for him to stop.

"Oh, brother," Barns sighed, swerving off the road and coming to a sudden stop. He rolled down his tinted window. "What do you need, boy?" he asked impatiently.

"Sir, I need a ride. Right away. Please…" The boy's voice was filled with anxiety, and Barns wondered if he was going to cry.

Barns paused a moment, considering his schedule and his plan to avoid all contact with people until the week's end. He sighed audibly. "All right," he said, opening the passenger door of his BMW. "Get in."

Appearing very upset, the boy nodded quickly and climbed into the car. "Straight ahead," he said urgently.

After a few moments of silence, the boy spoke again. "There, up ahead, turn right," he said.

"That's a dirt road," Barns said, frustrated by the boy. "Do you know what all that dust will do to my car, huh?" he asked.

The boy shook his head. "Please take it, sir. It leads to a paved road, I promise," he said quickly.

Barns followed the boy's directions, taking the dirt road until it turned into a paved road which began to wind up a mountainside.

"How far up?" Barns asked, glancing at the boy and wondering when he would find time to have his car washed again. Just as he had predicted moments earlier, the dirt road had covered the shiny black paint with a fine layer of light brown silt.

The boy pointed up the road. "Take this a few more miles to the top," he said.

Barns sighed aloud and drove in silence toward the mountaintop. As they approached it, Barns began to hear the faint sound of high-pitched screams. He was suddenly confused. "Where are we going?" he asked, looking strangely at the boy.

"To help," the boy said. "Hurry."

Barns drove a bit faster, something in his cold heart warmed slightly by the boy's attitude and a growing concern over the screaming sounds, which were growing louder by the minute. The boy held up his hand. "Stop here," he said. Then he pointed over to the edge of the road, which had no guard rail and led to a sharp drop-off, hundreds of feet down into a canyon.

Barns climbed out of his car and heard the sound clearly now. It was children, dozens of them screaming for help. Instantly, he ran toward the edge of the road and looked down. What he saw horrified him. There was a yellow school bus perched precariously on its side and resting on a ledge of rocks at least two hundred feet down the canyon. Barns turned around and ran back to his car with the little boy running alongside him.

Forgetting that it hadn't worked only thirty minutes earlier, Barns picked up his cellular telephone and dialed the number for emergency service. It worked instantly.

"Quick, send ambulances and paramedics," he said quickly. "A bus has flipped over the canyon and it's filled with children. I'm a doctor. I'll do my best until you get here."

Barns gave the dispatch operator specific directions to the site and then hung up the phone. He placed both hands on the shoulders of the little boy beside him and looked intently into his eyes. "Stay here," he said. "I'm going down the hill to help out."

The boy nodded and watched as Barns ran toward the road's edge and then disappeared over the side. The canyon was incredibly steep, but Barns was able to use rocks and vegetation to help make his way to the disabled bus. Children were reaching out the windows, screaming for help, and smoke was beginning to fill the cabin area.

"Lord, help me on this one," he prayed silently. And then he got to work.

He made his way carefully to the front of the bus, but the hydraulic doors were pinned shut against a jagged rock. He began to kick and push the rock until finally it fell away, tumbling violently down the steep canyon. Barns watched it fall and realized the rescue would have to be slow and cautious if he was to get any of the children up the hillside. One wrong move and he and the children would certainly fall to their deaths.

Just then, he heard the distant sound of sirens, and he was instantly thankful. He could begin helping the children out of the bus, but the effort would take several strong adults if it were to be successful. Barns was still trying to open the bus's doors when emergency personnel began filing cautiously down the hill.

"Everyone all right?" one of the paramedics yelled.

"Not sure," Barns responded. "They're real upset, and it's starting to fill up with smoke. We have to hurry."

"You the doctor who made the call?" the man asked, joining Barns at the bus's door.

"Yes."

"A fall like this one means lots of possible neck injuries, back injuries, that kind of thing," the paramedic said as others joined them, forming a human chain and carrying a thick cable from the road's edge to where the bus lay. Each child would be placed into a carrier, which would, in turn, be attached to the cable to prevent any of them from falling into the canyon.

"Let's hurry," the paramedic said.

Barns nodded. "We need to move carefully. The ground isn't very stable."

Ambulances were still arriving as Barns and the paramedic finally opened the bus doors and gently lifted out the nearest child. Barns did an initial check and deemed that the little girl miraculously had no neck or back injuries. The child was placed in a basket and handed from one paramedic to the next until she was safely at the top of the hill. There she was placed into an ambulance where paramedics immediately began checking the extent of her injuries.

Working together, Barns and the paramedics were able to take each of the twenty-five children from the bus and get them safely to the top of the hill. As time passed, Barns completely forgot about the little boy up on the road who was supposed to be waiting for him in his BMW. He was completely absorbed in the work at hand.

When it appeared that their efforts were finished, one of the paramedics climbed into the bus for a final look. Barns and the others watched from nearby, waiting for the signal that the bus was empty. Instead, the paramedic climbed out and shook his head, his face grim from what he'd just seen.

"One more," he shouted. "I'll need some help."

"How badly is he hurt?" Barns asked, moving toward the bus.

The paramedic shook his head, looking down at the ground. "He didn't make it," he said. "Just didn't make it."

Barns nodded, feeling the sting of tears in his eyes. As a doctor, he had never completely understood the gift he had of helping people overcome illness and injury until now. For the past hour, rescuing one crying child after another, Barns's heart had changed completely. He felt only a great sense of loss now that one of the children hadn't made it.

He moved carefully toward the bus. "I'll help," he said. Once inside, he followed closely behind the paramedic, climbing over the sides of one seat after another as they made their way to the back of the bus.

"He's over there," the paramedic said, pointing to a small corner near the bus's emergency door, which was pinned against the wall of the canyon.

"Looks like a broken neck," the paramedic said softly.

Barns moved into place and got a look at the limp body of the little boy who had been killed in the accident.

"No," he said. "It can't be." His voice was a haunting whisper as he rested back on his heels. His face grew startlingly pale as the paramedic stared at him strangely. After all, the man was a doctor and the paramedic did not expect him to react so strongly to the sight of a child's body. He had certainly seen death before.

"Are you OK?" the paramedic asked. "I can get someone else if this is too hard for you."

Barns shook his head violently. "It's *impossible*," he said, and the paramedic wondered if he were perhaps in shock because of the trauma of the lengthy rescue. "It's him."

"Do you know this boy?" the paramedic asked as he turned to look at the child.

"The little boy who brought me here," Barns said.

The paramedic wrinkled his brow in confusion. "I think you need some fresh air, Doc," he said. But Barns shook his head.

"I'm fine," he said. "Come on, let's get to work."

Barns knew it was impossible. But the still little body before him was the same boy who had been standing on the highway, the same boy who had given him directions up the hillside. He wore a scouting uniform and a red baseball cap. Barns was certain he was the same boy.

The paramedic watched Barns's reaction curiously and shrugged. "OK. We need to get him up the hill."

The men worked together to move the boy's body out of the bus and up the hill. As they worked, Barns wondered if he might have been mistaken. Perhaps the boys were twin brothers. There had to be an explanation. As they reached the road, Barns set the boy's body down and hurried across the road to his car. He had told the boy to stay in the car until he was finished. But as he approached it and opened the car door, he could see that the boy was gone.

"Hey," he yelled, running toward the fire captain who had overseen the entire operation from the road. "A little boy showed me where this accident was. I told him to wait for me in the car over there. Blond hair, blue eyes, red baseball cap, wearing a scouting uniform. Did you see where he went?"

The captain shook his head curiously. "Hasn't been anyone up here but us," he said. "When we got here, we checked that car, looking for whoever made the call. It was empty. Wasn't anyone up here at all."

Barns was incredulous. He moved away to a private spot on the road where he would be alone. He sat on the roadway and dropped his head into his hands. He replayed the incidents of the past two hours in his mind. The boy had definitely been real. He had waved him down and guided him toward the bus. Barns knew he never would have found the accident site if it hadn't been for the boy and his patient insistence that they drive to the top of the mountain.

Suddenly, Barns began to think the situation through. Until now he hadn't considered some of the obviously strange details surrounding the boy's appearance on the side of the highway. How had the boy walked more than five miles down the mountainside and out toward the highway by himself? If he had been in the bus, how had he escaped without any help? And how had he suddenly disappeared in the moments after Barns had made the emergency call? Most of all, who could explain the tiny covered body they'd brought up the hill? He looked identical to the child who had led him to the accident scene.

At that instant, chills ran the length of Dr. Barns's spine. When they passed, he was engulfed in a feeling of peace and a sudden understanding. Was it possible? Could the boy have been an angel, taking the image of the small little boy who had died in the accident? Barns closed his eyes and began crying. Perhaps God had hoped to teach him some kind of lesson here. Indeed, Barns knew with everything in him that he would never again be the same calloused man he had become. A person's life was so tenuous, so brief. But Barns knew he had been unable to see the value of the people behind his patients.

"Never again," Barns cried quietly, shaking his head in disgust at his former blindness. "Thank you, God. Whatever happened here, whoever that little boy was, thank you."

"You OK?" one of the paramedics asked as he approached him.

Barns nodded, wiping the tears from his face and standing up. "I need to see that boy once more," he said, moving past the paramedic toward the covered body several feet away. Gently he removed the tarp from his face, feeling the now familiar wave of shock. There was no doubt. He was the same boy. Barns bent down and softly brushed a lock of the child's blond hair back under his baseball cap.

"Goodbye, little boy," he whispered, fresh tears flooding his eyes. "Whoever you are, I thank you."

Have You Had
an Angel Encounter?

IF YOU WOULD LIKE TO SHARE A STORY involving an angel encounter—an unusual incident involving someone who seemed to be a real person until they disappeared or with someone who after further research never really existed—I would very much appreciate hearing from you. Your story may be used in an upcoming volume of angel encounters.

Please write a brief account of your experience, and include your name, address, telephone number, and other pertinent details of the encounter. If you would rather have your real name left out of the story, should it appear in print, please mention this in your letter. The author cannot guarantee that your story will be published, but your effort will be much appreciated all the same.

Address your angel encounters to:

Kelsey Tyler
P.O. Box 264
Clarkdale, Arizona 86324-9998